THE ULTIMATE
NEW YORK YANKEES
BASEBALL CHALLENGE

THE ULTIMATE
NEW YORK YANKEES
BASEBALL
CHALLENGE

David Nemec
and
Scott Flatow

TAYLOR TRADE PUBLISHING

Lanham • New York • Boulder • Toronto • Plymouth, UK

The authors would like to thank Al Blumkin and Dave Zeman for their help in fact-checking this book.

Copyright © 2007 by David Nemec and Scott Flatow
First Taylor Trade Publishing edition 2007

This Taylor Trade Publishing paperback edition of *The Ultimate New York Yankees Baseball Challenge* is an original publication. It is published by arrangement with the author.

Published by Taylor Trade Publishing
An imprint of The Rowman & Littlefield Publishing Group, Inc.
4501 Forbes Boulevard, Suite 200, Lanham, Maryland 20706

Distributed by NATIONAL BOOK NETWORK

Library of Congress Cataloging-in-Publication Data

Nemec, David.
    The ultimate New York Yankees baseball challenge / David Nemec and
Scott Flatow. — 1st Taylor Trade Publishing ed.
        p. cm.
    Includes bibliographical references and index.
    ISBN 1-58979-328-5 (pbk. : alk. paper)
    1. New York Yankees (Baseball team)—Miscellanea. I. Flatow, Scott,
1966- II. Title.
GV875.N4N46 2007
796.357'64097471—dc22   2006037813

©™ The paper used in this publication meets the minimum require-
ments of American National Standard for Information Sciences—
Permanence of Paper for Printed Library Materials, ANSI/NISO
Z39.48-1992.

Manufactured in the United States of America.

CONTENTS

GAME 4

GAME 5

GAME 6

GAME 7

INTRODUCTION

How dare we call this the ultimate New York Yankees base-ball challenge?

First and foremost, it's designed to give you, our dear reader, the four things you most want in a baseball quiz book: (1) pleasure; (2) a worthy challenge; (3) an opportunity to learn something new about the game you love and the team that, chances are, many of you either most love or else most love to hate; and (4) the assurance that you're in the company of quiz masters who know their stuff. In short, you not only want to match wits, you also like to come away from a book like this with the feeling that you've been enlightened in the bargain.

You will be, you have our guarantee, by the time you finish here. What we've assembled is a seven-game World Series of entertainment, innings one through nine, starting off with rookies and ending with famous Fall Classic events, heroes and villains. There's a logic to our structure, of course, as there is to all the categories we've chosen. In fact, we'll alert you right off the bat, as it were, that to score well against our curves, drops and heat you need to be moderately savvy in every on-the-field phase of the Yankees rich history from Hilltop Park to the present day.

That isn't to say, though, that you've got to have a raft of statistics and a host of obscure players at your fingertips. Actually, top marks are there for the taking by anyone who has a reasonable amount of knowledge of the game in general coupled with a good eye for using our clues to zero in on the right answer to even our seemingly most impossible questions.

Before ushering you behind the curtain and showing you how our minds work, first let us show you an example of the type of question we abhor: What Kansas City Royals batter hit into the first triple play in Seattle Mariners history and what Mariner recorded the last out in the play? Unless you happened to see that particular play (which is highly unlikely) or else have a PhD in triple plays (also unlikely), all you can do is throw up your hands and take a couple of wild guesses as to who the two players are. And how much fun is there in that? However, if the question had also provided the clues that the unlucky Royals batter now resides in the Hall of Fame and the Mariner who recorded the last out in the triple play spent most of his career as a backup catcher in the mid-1970s with the Astros, then all the burners would be fired and the question would be a fair one to ask, albeit still not one to our taste.

In a nutshell, that's our approach. A good question doesn't just toss up a mildly interesting but essentially arcane feat. It gives you a reasonable opportunity to nail the player or players who were involved in it by providing enough information about them to allow you to make at least an educated guess. Hall of Famer? Could be Harmon Killebrew who finished his career in KC. But wait! Was Killebrew still around when the Mariners came into existence? No. Then who was? We won't spoil the fun by giving away the answer any more than we'll spill on the 'stros backup catcher, but now you get the idea how we work.

Here we are cobbling away in our workshop on three different levels of questions that are more to our taste:

SIMPLE: Who held the Yankees season home run record prior to Roger Maris? Single.

INTERMEDIATE: What is the most recent Yankees World Series entrant to showcase at least one Hall of Fame performer? Careful, you won't win here if you get mired in the wrong year. RBI double.

EXPERT: Who was the only member of the 1941 Yankees to play for the Whiz Kids against the Yankees in the 1950 World Series? Learning that he was a catcher and later was a ML coach who finished the 1967 season at the helm of the Atlanta Braves will help experts score here. Three-run homer.

Question 1 is so easy that it merits no clues and rates only a single.

In question 2 you're given fair warning that it contains clues when it's read carefully. One clue is an effort to steer you away from an answer that is wrong and the other clue tries to direct you to the right answer. Good for you if you've already spotted that our clues sometimes come in the form of wordplay, puns or even anagrams.

The clues in question 3 are straightforward and the reward one of the highest offered in our book. In addition, you get a sampling of the standard abbreviations we use throughout the book. Here it's ML, short for major league. Elsewhere you'll encounter other standard abbreviations such as NL for National League, AL for American League, PCL for Pacific Coast League, LA for Los Angeles, KC for Kansas City, ABs for at bats, BA for batting average, SA for slugging average, ERA for earned run average, CG for complete games and OPS for on-base percentage plus slugging average.

We won't spoil your fun by giving away the answers to our sample questions. Consider them a bonus. And, incidentally, there are a number of other bonuses in our book, not the least of which is our invitation to compile your own BA, SA, RBI and total base totals as you cruise along. There are over 660 at bats in *The Ultimate New York Yankees Baseball Challenge* or about the same number you'd get in a season if you were in there for all 162 games. Don't expect to hit above .300, though, unless you really know your Yankees. But by the same token, you have our assurance that not even diehard Yankees fans are likely to outhit readers that have a firm knowledge of all of major league history. This, after all, is the ultimate Yankees test for the ultimate well-rounded fan.

One final note. The statistics in our books in rare cases will differ from those in other reference works and even in a few instances from those accepted by Major League Baseball. An example is Roger Maris's RBI total in 1961. Most reference works continue to credit Maris with 142 RBI and the undisputed American League leadership. However, reliable research has documented that Maris had only 141 RBI in 1961, tying him with Jim Gentile for the AL RBI crown. There are other such occasions when we might present data that is slightly ahead of the curve. But there are no occasions in this book when the correct answer to a question rides on conflicting data.

Now enjoy.

FOREWORD

I am honored to write the foreword for this groundbreaking series of baseball quiz books by Scott Flatow and David Nemec. I first encountered Scott at the Society for American Baseball Research (SABR) New York City regional meeting in 1985. He wrote an especially challenging and compelling baseball quiz for the event, which I consider myself very fortunate to have won. We became close friends soon after that meeting. Scott quickly went on to bigger and better things as both a baseball trivia player and an author. In recent years he has won three SABR National Trivia championships (two team and one individual). Scott's 1995 team set the current SABR team record for the widest margin of victory, and he later posted the highest individual score to date when he won the individual competition in 2001. During that span he also co-authored *The Macmillan Baseball Quiz Book* and penned *The McFarland Baseball Quiz Book*. In addition, he has written numerous quizzes for independent publications.

In 1991, Scott received a call from Steve Nadel, the New York City SABR chapter chairman and host of that year's National convention in New York City, informing him that David Nemec was planning to attend a SABR convention for the first time. Scott immediately contacted me and we both became very excited because David is recognized to be the father of baseball trivia. He had written two books in the late 1970s, *The Absolutely Most Challenging Baseball Quiz Book, Ever* and *The Even More Challenging Baseball Quiz Book*, that are now regarded as the pioneering works in the field. Scott and I first met David in June of 1991 at the SABR New York City National convention for which Scott orchestrated the trivia competition. As a first-time player, David helped his team to narrowly defeat my team in the finals, and an instant bond developed between us.

In addition to *The Absolutely Most Challenging Baseball Quiz Book, Ever* and *The Even More Challenging Baseball Quiz Book*, David is the author of more than 25 baseball books including two quiz books in the 1990s, the indispensable *The Great Encyclopedia of Nineteenth Century Major League Baseball* and *The Beer and Whisky League*, which ranks as the seminal work on the American Association in the years that it was a major league. David is also the co-holder with me of a record seven SABR National Trivia Championships. He has won six team competitions as well as the first individual championship in 1995.

The matchless qualities in David Nemec's and Scott Flatow's new series of team quiz books are their wry wit, their amazing scope and, above all, the fact that they not only test a reader's recall, they also force him or her to think out of the box and in so doing to expand his or her knowledge of our national game. You will never find such tired posers as "Who pitched the only perfect game in the World Series?" or "What year did the Dodgers move to Los Angeles?" Instead you will be constantly challenged to test the depth and breadth of your baseball knowledge from the first major league baseball game in 1871 to the present day. Furthermore, in this unique series of quiz books you are certain to learn a wealth of new information about players ranging from the well known like Babe Ruth and Hank Aaron to such inimitably ephemeral performers as Eddie Gaedel and Shooty Babbit.

In short, Nemec and Flatow inform as well as entertain. Most other quiz books are content to lob questions at you without helping to guide you toward the answer. You either know who hit such and such, or you don't. Your only recourse if you don't is to consult the answer section, shrug and move on. Nemec and Flatow take a very different approach. First they toss a tantalizing and oftentimes completely original teaser to set your synapses firing. Then they crank your brain up to full boil with descriptive clues that are deftly designed to steer the savvy mind toward the answer. And fair warning: the answer is all too often a name that will make you whack your forehead and go, "Wow, how did I ever miss that?" Have fun with these books. I never had so much fun in all my long years as a trivia aficionado.

Alan Blumkin is the only man to win two consecutive individual SABR National trivia championships. In addition, he has made numerous historical presentations at both local and National SABR conventions. He lives in Brooklyn, New York, and is currently resting on his laurels while serving as the chief administrator and question contributor for the annual SABR National championships.

GAME 1

INNING 1
RED-HOT ROOKIES

1 Who is the lone Yankees hurler to start a World Series game in the same season that he won Rookie of the Year honors? After posting a 2.05 ERA in 15 starts, this lefty started Game 3 of the Series but did not receive a decision as the Yanks lost 5-4. Just a single, plus a RBI for the year.

2 The first Yankee to cop a Rookie of the Year Award edged out a rival AL rookie who led him in almost every offensive department, triggering charges from other AL teams that the voters were biased. Both men had substantial careers in the majors, but the Yankee played in numerous World Series while his rival never saw postseason action. Name both of these frosh stars for a triple; sac hit if you know just the Yankees award winner.

3 He led all Yankees regulars in batting at .302 and placed second on the club in OPS (.801) while topping the majors at his position in assists. No surprise that he trounced the competition in that year's AL Rookie of the Year poll, sweeping every vote but one, which went to Cleveland's Roy Foster. One base for him and a RBI for the year he did it.

4 The last player summoned directly from Class D ball to the majors was this starter-reliever who posted an eye-popping 15-1 slate with Auburn in the New York-Penn League. Continuing his success up top, he went 11-5 with two shutouts for Houk's crew in 1961. It was all downhill for him thereafter, but you can lift yourself up with a RBI double.

5 Who is the lone man to win 20 games for the Yankees in the only season he pitched in enough innings to qualify for an ERA title? We'll furnish the clues that he did it as a rookie and that the his final win in his eight-year career came with the 1960 St. Louis Cardinals and still donate a double to your column if you can solve this mystery.

6 Who holds the Yankees all-time record for the most wins by a rookie? RBI double.

7 His 2.05 frosh ERA is the third lowest among Yankees hurlers, freshman or not, who logged as many as 250 innings in a season since 1920. Winner of 17 games as a rookie, this native of Council Bluffs, Iowa, easily copped top AL yearling honors. Score a single, plus a RBI for the year.

8 The lone hurler in history to lead the AL both in saves and ERA as a frosh was a Yankee. Name him and put a double in your column, plus an extra base for the year he did it.

9 At age 23, he set the current Yankees rookie mark with 55 hill appearances while serving as the righty closing half of their pen and posting 14 saves with a 2.38 ERA in just under 100 innings. The first Yankee born in Hawaii, he said Aloha with the Mariners in 1992. RBI single.

10 What lefty hitter set the current Yankees mark for the highest batting average by a rookie in his second season with the club after losing most of what otherwise would have been his official rookie year to a broken ankle? Double, plus a RBI for the year he set the mark.

AB: 10
Hits: 10
Total Bases: 18
RBI: 7

INNING 2
WHAT WAS THEIR REAL HANDLE?

We know these Yankees today by their nicknames or, in some cases, their middle names. By what first names did their mothers know them?

1 Babe Ruth. Looping single—you need both the first and middle names here to score.

2 Ken Griffey, Sr. RBI single.

3 Chuck Knoblauch. Double.

4 Bubba Crosby. Double.

5 Red Rolfe. Take two bases.

6 Red Ruffing. RBI single.

7 Whitey Ford. Infield single.

8 Mike Stanton. Bases clearing double.

9 Wid Conroy. Nobody said the pitching wouldn't get tougher—two-run homer.

10 Chick Fewster. Two-run shot.

11 Shane Spencer. Another three-run two-bagger.

12 Dooley Womack. Triple.

> **AB**: 12
> **Hits**: 12
> **Total Bases**: 25
> **RBI**: 12

INNING 3
MASTER MOUNDSMEN

1 The first Yankee to lead the AL in wins is also the club record holder for most victories in a season. Routine single.

2 The most recent Yankee to win 20 games in back-to-back seasons is worth a single, but add a RBI for pegging both years he reached the charmed circle.

3 Between 1911 and 1963 only one Yankees hurler fanned as many as 200 batters in a season. Name him for a double, plus a RBI for the year he reached the 200 plateau.

4 The pitcher who holds the Yankees club mark for consecutive seasons with as many as 200 innings also sports their record for the most successive campaigns with as many as 20 complete games. RBI single.

5 What Yankee will in all probability be the last hurler in big league history to complete 30 games in a season? That year was his first in pinstripes but his fifth consecutive 20-win season. Single for him and a RBI for the year.

6 Who won the most career games for the Yanks while posting an overall losing record in pinstripes? From 1910–1919, he went 95-99 including 19 wins in 1915 while placing second in complete games to Walter Johnson with 31. Triple.

7 After signing with the Yanks as a free agent, he led the AL in winning percentage (.750), and for an encore he boosted that figure to .818 and topped the league in victories. By that time his record stood at 35-10 in pinstripes, but rotator cuff surgery stalled him at age 34. Although he returned for a few seasons, this lefty was never again nearly as effective. RBI single.

8 Who was the last man to pitch on Yankees, Dodgers and Giants pennant winners while all three teams were still based in New York? Double if you know the NL's surprise MVP runner-up in 1956.

9 What Yankees hurler topped the AL in Ks three times even though he never struck out as many as 200 batters in a season? RBI single.

10 Who is the most recent Yankees righty to win 20 games in a season while posting an ERA below 3.00? Thereafter, an elbow injury limited him to just seven more victories after he'd notched 55 in his previous three Bronx campaigns. Single, plus a RBI for the year he won 20.

AB: 10
Hits: 10
Total Bases: 14
RBI: 6

INNING 4
GOLD GLOVE GOLIATHS

1 Not only was he the initial Yankees Gold Glove recipient, this hurler also won the honor in each of the first four years it was given in the AL and ran that streak to eight after moving to the NL. Double.

2 The first Yankees position player to win a Gold Glove was this outfielder that hit .300 and grabbed a World Championship ring that season. Easy to get burned here, as did he sometimes while playing the "sun field," so we'll bid a triple, plus a RBI for the year he flashed his leather.

3 The first Yankees fly hawk to field 1.000 (minimum 100 games) in a season served his entire career with the Bombers. Although he played on three straight pennant winners, the first didn't come until his 12th campaign in the Bronx. RBI single, plus an extra base for the year he fielded flawlessly.

4 Prior to expansion when the schedule was lengthened to 162 games, what Yankee held the ML record for the most games at first base in two consecutive seasons after playing 157 games in back-to-back years? Deductive reasoning alone should bring you a single.

5 In 1938 Joe DiMaggio recorded 21 assists, but at the time there was no Gold Glove to honor him. Since then, only one Yankees outfielder gunned down as many runners as DiMag did in 1938. Nevertheless he failed to cop the top fielding award that year, although he did net his lone Gold Glove two seasons earlier. Double and a RBI for the year he won the award.

6 There are enough clues here to run down the name of the Yankees first sacker who holds not only the AL record but also the NL record for the most chances accepted, excluding errors, in a doubleheader in which both games lasted the regulation nine innings. RBI double.

7 Better known for his bat than his glove, he nevertheless set an all-time AL record when he logged 11 assists at third base on May 24, 1918, in a 3-2 loss to Cleveland at the Polo Grounds that took 19 innings. The clue that earlier in his career he had played at the Polo Grounds in the uniform of another AL team shaves this to only a double.

8 Only one Yankee who played a certain position ever copped a Gold Glove in pinstripes and he's also the first Bomber to snag five awards total. Our sharing that his first four Gold Gloves came with pennant winners reduces this to a RBI single, but to score it you need both him and the position that has been graced by only one Gold Glove, his.

9 Who was the first man to play shortstop for the Yankees in two consecutive World Series and also the first shortstop to lead the AL in fielding average eight consecutive seasons? Rates only a RBI double.

10 What shortstop–second base duo set an all-time Yankees season record when they participated in 260 double plays combined? Telling you they also hold the record for the most seasons collectively as baseball broadcasters who were a former keystone combo knocks this down to just a single. Add a RBI if you nail the year they set the DP record after learning it was the last season a World Series was played in which no African Americans participated.

AB: 10
Hits: 10
Total Bases: 18
RBI: 7

INNING 5
RBI RULERS

1 What Yankee was the only AL switch hitter to drive in 100 runs in 2003? RBI single.

2 Babe Ruth led the Yanks in RBI during each of his first five seasons in pinstripes. Who was the only other Bomber to achieve this feat as many as four straight times after coming to the Bronx from another club? His impact in the Big Apple was too great for us to offer more than a bunt single.

3 Who failed to lead the club in RBI during any of his four 100-ribby campaigns with the Bombers but had earlier topped the team in consecutive years with lackluster totals of 83 and 96? Adding that his club leaderships came in strike-shortened seasons makes this only a single.

4 Who was the first member of the Yankees to notch as many as 100 RBI in a season? Not as hard as it might appear. RBI single, plus an extra ribby for the year.

5 The first Yankees third baseman to plate 100 RBI did it just once in over 20 years under the big top. Slow-rolling single, but add a RBI for the year.

6 Who led the first New York AL team in 1903 with 82 RBI, a club record that stood until 1911? The clue that he is still the owner of the all-time rookie record for triples reduces this to a two-run double.

7 Who holds the Yankees all-time record for the most RBI in a season with 0 home runs? Home run.

8 When Derek Jeter logged 102 RBI in 1999, he became only the second Yankees shortstop to top 100 ribbies. Who still holds the club season record for the most RBI by a shortstop with 107? RBI triple, plus an extra ribby for the year he set the mark.

9 What Yankee knocked in 100 ribbies on less than 10 home runs in back-to-back seasons in the 1920s? Triple

10 During the 1990s, two right-handed batters drove in 100 runs in a season with the Yanks. One's a cinch, but the other's a little trickier so we'll add that he served as their primary DH that year. One base for each.

AB: 10
Hits: 10
Total Bases: 19
RBI: 7

INNING 6
TEAM TEASERS

1 It's become increasingly rare for a team to flaunt two 20 game winners. The last time the Yanks did it they won the pennant. Grab a single for the year and a RBI for each of their 20-win twirlers.

2 The 1912 Yankees club did not have a single Hall of Famer on its roster all year. What was the next season the Yanks failed to feature at least one future Cooperstown inductee on their roster? Mine your mental rolodex of Yankees teams and reason this one out for a double. It's not as hard as it might appear.

3 What Yankees crew was leading the AL on June 1 and then went into a 31-88 tailspin that sunk them deep into the cellar at the season's end? We'll tell you that dissension was blamed for the club's tumble and the player-manager who took over the reins near the end of June was made the scapegoat, and then we'll still award a two-run homer for the year, plus an extra ribby for the manager that finished the season at the Yankees helm.

4 Identify the year that the Yanks led the AL in steals with 251, their .223-hitting shortstop led the team in homers with a mere three, and rightfielder Doc Cook rapped .283 to earn the honor of being the Yankees top batting title qualifier. Triple for the year, two RBI for the "slugging" shortstop.

5 Rare is the year that a team wins the Triple Crown—leading its league in BA, FA and ERA—and fails to also win the pennant. Rarer yet is the club that finishes ahead of a team Triple Crown winner and neglects to capture the flag. In fact, there is only one such club in all of major league history, and that team, alas, is a New York AL entry. What year are we describing and what team won the AL flag that year? Two bases for the year and one for the flag winner.

6 What Yankees team featured a starting pitcher that had the worst won-lost record of any ERA qualifier in AL history that hurled for a pennant winner? We will toss in the clues that two years earlier he had led the Yanks in wins with 13 and that the season in question he owned the worst won-lost record in major league history of any pitcher to start a World Series game when he took the mound in what proved to be one of the most exciting contests in postseason history. We will even reveal that he lost the game on the last pitch he ever threw in the majors as a starting pitcher and still grant a double for the year and a RBI for the pitcher.

7 Whoa now! Name the club that won the most games of any Yankees team that Casey Stengel managed. Double for the year and a RBI for the team the Yanks faced that season in the Series.

8 The club that had the worst record of any Yankees team that Casey Stengel piloted had one glaring weakness. Uncharacteristically, the team couldn't hit and tallied just 687 runs. What year was it and who topped the club in RBI with just 75? Double for the year, plus a RBI for the ribby leader.

9 The stolen base has not usually been a major weapon among Yankees pennant winners, but this flag bearer featured three Bombers who each swiped over 30 sacks. Knowing they were swept in the Series that season still nets you one base for each, plus a RBI for the year.

10 What Yankees world champ was the first team in big league history to feature three outfielders that each clubbed as many as 30 homers? Score a double for the year and a RBI for each of their fly hawks.

AB: 10
Hits: 10
Total Bases: 24
RBI: 14

INNING 7
HOME RUN KINGS

1 Who was the first Yankee to top the AL in homers? Double.

2 An outfielder who set a team record with five dingers that lasted all of one year paced the New York AL club in homers in 1903, its first year of existence in the Big Apple. Who was he for a two-run homer?

3 In 1919 the Yankees led the AL with 45 homers. The following year Babe Ruth arrived and promptly hit more homers than the entire 1919 team. In the Yanks last pre-Ruth season, what former AL home run king topped the club with 10 taters? Double.

4 After leading the AL in homers, what Yankees slugger hiked his home run total the following season by five but failed to repeat as tater champ? RBI double.

5 Joe DiMaggio missed the first half of the season in 1949 with a stubborn bone spur in his heel but still led all Yanks outfielders with 14 homers. Who paced the entire team with 24 homers? RBI double.

6 The year after playing on a Bombers world champ, he socked a homer against the Yanks with a team that defeated them in the Fall Classic. No slouch in October, he clubbed seven round-trippers for the Yankees in Series play. Double, but you'll need both the team and year our man turned the tables on the Yanks to grab an extra base.

7 Red Ruffing easily leads all Yankees pitchers in career home runs with 31. The man who is second with 11 was a frequent pinch hitter during his two stints with the Bombers during the 1940s and 1950s.

8 Who pounded over 20 homers in each of his first two seasons in pinstripes but retired with the fewest career games played in the majors by a slugger with as many as two 20-dinger campaigns? Just a single.

9 Who held the Yankees record for homers in a season by a shortstop prior to Derek Jeter? Please don't say Tom Tresh, who hit 20 in 1962 but five came while playing in left field. The Yanks acquired our man early in the season, and he too poked 20 seat-reachers, but only four came at other positions. Double for him, and a RBI for the year, plus an extra base for the club with which he started the season.

10 What Yankee slammed a ML record 14 homers against one team in a single season? Double for him, an extra base for the year plus a RBI for the club he victimized.

AB: 10
Hits: 10
Total Bases: 24
RBI: 7

INNING 8
ALL IN THE FAMILY

1 In his first season with the Yanks, he paced them in homers, RBI, slugging, walks, OBP and OPS, as his younger brother poled 20 taters while splitting duty with two other ML clubs. The year before, the pair combined to slam 73 doubles as teammates for a club that won 102 games. Nail both sibs for a single, plus a RBI for the team on which they played together.

2 A former AL MVP with another club, he later teamed with his brother on a Yankees pennant winner after playing two seasons with him as a batterymate on their previous outfit. Double for the family name, an extra base for both their first names, plus a RBI for the year they joined forces on the Yanks.

3 What Yankees gardener and his brother missed by one year becoming the first pair of siblings to face each other in a World Series? RBI single, plus an extra base for the year it happened.

4 Knowing the first member of the Yankees to father a son that played with the New York Giants earns our admiration in the form of a grand slam homer.

5 Who were the only position-playing brothers to be teammates on the Yankees in the same season? Knowing they earlier teamed with a third brother on another club and that one of them fathered a son who once hit over .350 in the NL makes this a cinch single for the family name. Stretch it to a double only if you name all four family members.

6 This New York AL first sacker never played in a 20th century World Series, but he did hit a famous home run in Yankees annals and his brother caught for the 1887 NL World Series representative. The family name rates a triple, plus a RBI for both of these brothers' first names.

7 A congenital back defect shortened this Yank's otherwise brilliant career and prevented his son from ever having one, but his brother caught briefly for the Senators in the 1950s. Take a double for the family name.

8 He won 16 games for the 1932 World Champs while his brother was toiling in five games for Brooklyn. It was his brother's only taste of the bigs, but the Yankees hurler had earlier logged a 20-win season and later became an umpire. RBI double for the family name.

9 In 1927 he caught for the St. Louis Browns while his brother was also catching in Sportsman's Park for the Cardinals, but earlier in their careers both siblings had played for teams in two different leagues that made the Polo Grounds their home. The older brother broke in with the 1914 Pirates and the younger with the 1913 A's. Between them they collected 1,541 regular season hits, but the younger sib made over 1,500, many of them in Yankees attire. The family name alone will win you a two-bagger.

10 While he was creaming Triple A pitching in the mid-1950s his brother was patrolling the outfield for the Red Sox and Senators. However, he played on a Yankees World Championship team in his rookie season in the bigs, a treat his brother never enjoyed. Both these sibs finished their careers with expansion teams—his brother very quietly but he with an éclat that earned him his famous nickname. The family name will buy you just a single, but an extra base for knowing the first names of both these sibs.

11 Some say he had the best control of any lefty ever, and all the books say he won 15 games for the first New York AL entry and nearly 200 all told. Oddly, he never competed in a World Series even though he played on three 20th century pennant winners, but his brother played in the 1906 Fall Classic. Name this southpaw star for a three-bagger; his brother rates a RBI.

AB: 11
Hits: 11
Total Bases: 26
RBI: 10

INNING 9
FALL CLASSICS

1 Although the Yankees have gone through many personnel changes since their World Championship in 1996, two men have played in every World Series game managed by Joe Torre. Two bases for both, zilch for just one.

2 In the Yankees first World Series appearance, their ace pitcher was considered by many to be the goat when the Yanks lost in eight games to the New York Giants. It's true that after winning the Series opener the ace dropped his next two starts to finish with a 1-2 record, but it's highly debatable that he was to blame in either of his losses. In the 26 innings he pitched in the 1921 Series, he allowed just 20 hits, walked none and gave up a mere five earned runs to finish with a glittering 1.73 ERA. What pitcher are we depicting here? RBI single.

3 Three Hall of Famers have patrolled center field for the Yankees in World Series action, and Bernie Williams may one day be a fourth. A two-run homer is yours if you know who played center for the Yankees in all eight games in their very first World Series appearance and was the initial Bomber ever to bat in a World Series game. Even knowing he wore Yanks livery in six different seasons and broke in with the 1912 Cardinals won't be a bit of help to any but the experts.

4 Who bagged two wins, including the clincher in the 2000 Subway Series? In so doing, this lefty became the first pitcher to notch a Fall Classic victory at both Yankee and Shea Stadiums. Double.

5 Who was the first man to play for the Yankees in a World Series game and later manage against them in a Fall Classic? Double.

6 Few men even today can brag that they played on a team that lost to the Yankees in a World Series and later played for a Bombers World Series winner. What second sacker was able to make that boast in October of 1947 after being a member earlier in his career of a club that was swept by the Yanks in its first World Series appearance in 20 years? His name will net a triple, plus a RBI for his NL Series club.

7 Who was the first player in modern World Series history (since 1903) to record his initial big league plate appearance in World Series action? Reasoning alone should lead you to his position, and adding that his entire 14-year career was spent in the Bronx should edge you closer to his name. One base.

8 A bum knee kept Babe Ruth on the bench for most of the 1921 Series and he followed by hitting just .118 in the 1922 Classic. In 1923, however, the Babe was in peak form as he played all six postseason games and hit .368. What teammate of the Babe's ripped Giants' pitching for a .417 BA to lead all hitters in the 1923 affair and make a strong case for being the Yankees first MVP in fall competition? RBI double.

9 During the Yanks 1999 Series sweep over the Braves only one Bomber cranked two homers and he hit both in the same game. The second blast was a walk-off shot in the 10th giving the Yankees a 6-5 victory and a commanding 3-0 Series lead. Take two for this forgotten outfielder.

10 What Yankees backup infielder replaced an injured Willie Randolph in a Fall Classic and led all regulars on either side with a .438 average? Double for him and an extra base for naming the teammate who beat him out for the 1978 Series MVP by batting .417 with 10 hits and seven RBI.

11 Be forewarned: This rates as one of the most challenging Yankees questions you'll face in our book. In the eight seasons between 1921 and 1928, five men caught as many as 100 career games in pinstripes. Each of the five appeared in at least one World Series with the Bombers, and we're betting a grand slam that not more than one of our readers in 50,000 can name all five; in fact we'll award a solo homer to those who know only four.

AB: 11
Hits: 11
Total Bases: 23
RBI: 6

GAME 2

INNING 1
STELLAR STICKWIELDERS

1 Who was the first member of the Yankees to win an AL batting crown? Rates a double, plus a RBI for the year.

2 Who is the only player to collect 200 hits in a season as a Yankee but finish with less than 1,000 career hits? We'll chip in the clue that he topped the AL in hits two seasons in a row in Yankees garb and award a RBI double, plus an extra RBI for the two years he led the junior loop in hits.

3 Ruth and Gehrig both posted seasons of 100 walks and 200 hits. We'll ante a triple that you'll struggle to name the only other man to do so in pinstripes, plus a RBI for the year he did it.

4 Who was the first man to win an AL batting crown the same year he played on a Yankees flag winner? Double, plus a RBI for the year.

5 Between Mickey Mantle in 1962 and Jason Giambi in 2003, only one Yankee led the AL in walks. That year, he coaxed 119 free passes but never drew more than 95 at any other time in his 18-year career. He bowed out with the Mets, and you can depart with a RBI single.

6 When Mark Koenig hit .319 in 1928, whose Yankees club record did he break for the highest season batting average by a shortstop (minimum 400 at bats)? Two-run homer.

7 Prior to Bernie Williams, who was the last switch-hitting batting title qualifier to hit .300 for the Bombers? Even after we tell you that he also struck .307 the previous year with the 1981 flag-winners, this gardener still merits a RBI double.

8 Easy to go wrong here, so reflect a moment. Who is the only Yankee to stroke as many as 100 doubles over the course of two consecutive seasons? Two-bagger of your own.

9 Who holds the Yankees club record for the highest batting average in a season by a second baseman (minimum 400 bats)? Double for him, extra base for the year he set the mark.

10 The most recent Yankees pitcher to hit .300 (minimum 50 at bats) for a full season went 16-8 on a Bombers world champ and slapped 20 hits in 64 tries. Interestingly, those offensive numbers were far out of character, as he hit just .183 in 328 career at bats with eight clubs, finishing with the Mets. Single, plus a RBI for the year he ripped opposing hurlers.

11 If we tell you that the Yankees record holder for the fewest strikeouts in a season by a batting title qualifier played in just one World Series with the Bombers and it came exactly a dozen years after he appeared in a World Series as a rookie shortstop with another AL team, can you snare a RBI double here?

> **AB**: 11
> **Hits**: 11
> **Total Bases**: 22
> **RBI**: 11

INNING 2
HEROES AND GOATS

1 What Yankee brought the 1926 World Series to an igno-
minious end when he was caught trying to steal second base
with two out in the ninth inning of the seventh and deciding
game and the Yanks cleanup hitter at the plate? Two-run single for the goat, plus an extra base for the cleanup hitter.

2 Sometimes being a one-man gang is not enough as this
Yankee proved when he heroically led both teams with nine hits
but still suffered the indignity of a Series sweep. Two bases.

3 In Game 7 of the 1952 World Series, who saved the
Yankees 4-2 win in the seventh inning when he made a last-
instant, knee-high grab of Jackie Robinson's bases-loaded
pop fly near the mound that seemed certain to drop safely
and score at least two runs to tie that game? After we tell
you that he was also a hero in the following year's World
Series when he led the Yanks in hitting with a .500 BA, we
can award only a RBI single.

4 This righty reliever must have literally been part goat as
every Diamondback smelled his deliveries in Game 6 of the
2001 World Series. In $1\frac{1}{3}$ innings he yielded ten hits and
nine runs to bury the Bombers after a weak start by Andy
Pettitte. Never again seen in pinstripes, he's a double.

5 What star hurler ended all hope that the 1904 AL pennant would fly over New York's Hilltop Park the following
year when he wild-pitched home the winning run that gave
Boston the AL flag on the final day of the 1904 season? He's
in the Hall of Fame, but all who fail to collect a single here
belong in the Hall of Shame.

6 The Yankees overcame his 1-for-19 showing to defeat a
club in six games that they had beaten 38 years earlier when

that outfit was located in another city. Dealt during the following year, his .236 composite average was more than 100 points below what he hit the previous regular season in pinstripes. Double, plus a RBI for the year he sank in the Series.

7 Name the pitcher that kept the Yanks faint World Series hopes alive one year by hurling a shutout in Game 5 and then stunned the baseball world by saving Game 6 in relief and coming out of the pen again the following day in the third inning of Game 7 to get the win that sealed the greatest comeback triumph in Yankees postseason history. The only additional clue we'll provide is that it happened when a Republican president occupied the White House. Single and a RBI for the year.

8 Despite his collecting just a measly single in 21 at bats, the Yanks still won the Series against a club that had defeated them the year before. Five years later he went just 3-for-16 in fall action with a Bombers Series loser but outhit the team by 17 points (.188 to .171). Double, plus a RBI for nailing both years.

9 He led all Yankees regulars with a .406 average and set a new Series record for hits (later tied) but couldn't prevent the Pinstripers from losing their second consecutive Fall Classic. Take a single for him, plus a RBI for the year, and add an extra base for knowing his hit total.

10 In the 1960 World Series, the Yankees set tons of batting records in a losing effort. What pitcher contributed heavily to the Yanks shocking defeat by being kayoed by Pittsburgh hitters in the first inning of Game 1 and in the second inning of Game 5, causing him to post a hideous 21.60 Series ERA to go with his two losses in just 1⅓ innings of work? Triple.

AB: 10
Hits: 10
Total Bases: 18
RBI: 7

INNING 3
CY YOUNG SIZZLERS

1 Who is the only Yankees hurler to win both a Rookie of the Year and a Cy Young Award? Simple single.

2 He never led the AL in wins, but he once had a season that saw him pace the junior loop in shutouts, Ks and ERA while recording 20 wins and six saves as well as what many regard as a retrospective Cy Young Award. It proved to be his lone 20-victory season in a career that saw him win a remarkable 131 of 191 decisions after he came to New York from the Tribe. RBI single.

3 In his second full season, he truly blossomed, winning his first 13 decisions. By the season's end, he paced the AL in wins, winning percentage and ERA but finished second in strikeouts, 12 behind Nolan Ryan. Not surprisingly, he won the Cy Young in a rout. Cinch single.

4 For a gift-wrapped single with ribbons and bows, name the oldest Yankee to win Cy Young honors.

5 The first of his two 20-win seasons with the Yankees brought him the AL lead in victories, winning percentage, shutouts and ERA along with a retrospective Cy Young Award and a winning World Series share. RBI double.

6 He topped the AL in wins, ERA and Ks and would have been an almost certain Cy Young winner had there been such an award the year that Charlie Gehringer won his lone batting title. Single and a RBI for the year.

7 After winning a disputed ERA crown in his rookie year with the Yanks, he celebrated his second season by pacing the AL in winning percentage and shutouts while posting the best overall stats of any pitcher in the junior loop exactly 14 years before the Cy Young Award was originated. RBI triple.

8 Among pitchers who debuted since the inception of the Cy Young Award, what hurler won the most career games with the Bombers without ever receiving a single Cy Young vote? Dominating the competition, he outdistances his nearest rival by more than 50 victories. Double, plus a RBI for coming within five of his career victory total.

9 Called the Curveless Wonder, he topped the AL with 27 wins, making him a probable retrospective Cy Young winner the year the Hitless Wonders won the World Series. Solo homer.

10 The Yankees experienced a long stretch when their hurlers barely received even token consideration come Cy Young time. In fact, from 1962 through 1974, only once did a Bomber garner so much as a single vote. Tough enough to award a double for him, plus a RBI for the year.

AB: 10
Hits: 10
Total Bases: 18
RBI: 7

INNING 4
BRAZEN BASE THIEVES

1 Who was the first Yankee to smack 30 homers and swipe 30 bases in a season? It was this slugging speedster's only season in the Bronx, and one of his finest as he posted the second highest OPS (.888) of his 14-year career. Take two, plus a ribby for the year in question.

2 An injury in 1987 thwarted Rickey Henderson in his bid to become only the second Yankee to lead the AL in thefts three straight years. Who was the first? RBI single.

3 What backstopper still holds the Bombers record for career steals by a receiver with 62 even though in his eight seasons in Yankees garb he played only 617 games and left the majors with a career BA of just .232? We'll even tell you he debuted with the 1908 club and still award a three-run shot.

4 No Yankee topped the AL in thefts between the end of World War II and Rickey Henderson's acquisition in 1985. What Bombers Hall of Famer came the closest to a theft title during that span, falling just two swipes short of the leader? Double.

5 Who is the only Yankee to lead the AL in both triples and stolen bases in the same season? We'll add that he did it with as many as 20 of each not one but *two* successive seasons and still award a two-bagger, plus a RBI for the years he did it.

6 What Yankees third sacker hit just .239 the year he paced the AL with 74 steals? Home run.

7 Who led a Yankees World Championship team with 17 regular-season steals but was caught 21 times? While in pinstripes he snagged 110 bases and got nailed 118 times, the worst career percentage among Bombers who reached the century mark in swipes since caught stealing stats were officially kept. Double.

8 Who was the first Yankee to lead the AL in thefts after the advent of the Lively Ball Era in 1920? RBI double.

9 We know better than to ask you the name of the Yankees record-holder for steals in a season. But for a single, can you tell us within two how many sacks he pilfered? Grab an extra base if you can tell us within two how many attempts he made and a RBI for the year his legs put him in the Bombers record book.

10 After nearly becoming the Yankees first loop theft king with 44 steals in 1905, just two behind AL leader Danny Hoffman, what outfielder retired at age 30 to devote full-time to his law practice? Two-run homer.

11 Who holds the record for the most consecutive years with as many as one stolen base in Yankees livery? RBI single.

AB: 11
Hits: 11
Total Bases: 26
RBI: 12

INNING 5
WHO'D THEY COME UP WITH?

All of these men were important contributors to Yankees history after beginning their careers with other major league teams. Do you know what their original clubs were? Take two extra RBI if you also know their debut seasons.

1 Steve Hamilton. Homer.

2 Jack Chesbro. RBI double.

3 Lou Piniella. Homer.

4 Red Ruffing. Double.

5 Graig Nettles. RBI single.

6 Carl Mays. Three-bagger.

7 Johnny Mize. RBI Double.

8 Ed Figueroa. Double.

9 George McQuinn. Two-run homer.

10 Ed Lopat. Three-bagger.

11 Willie Randolph. RBI double.

12 Tommy John. Double.

> **AB**: 12
> **Hits**: 12
> **Total Bases**: 31
> **RBI**: 33

INNING 6
FAMOUS FEATS

1 What Yankee knocked home an AL record 11 runs in a 25-2 win over the Philadelphia A's on May 24, 1936? Just a single.

2 The first performer in big league history to homer in two consecutive pinch-hit appearances was a Yankee but not Ruth or Gehrig. In fact, he wasn't even a position player! Will lightning strike you as it once, literally, struck this pitcher while on the mound in the years after he hit consecutive pinch-hit blasts on June 10 and 11 in 1915? Two-run triple.

3 He tied a major league record on August 17, 1944, when he drilled four consecutive doubles in one game. In his rookie campaign he made 23 mound appearances. Both of these feats came while he was in pinstripes. For a RBI double who is he?

4 The lone Yankee to make six hits in a game prior to expansion did it in 1934. We'll add that he finished his major league career with the 1945 Indians and later became a pitching star in the Florida International League and still award a two-run triple.

5 Unless the rules change so that AL pitchers bat against rival AL teams, a Yankees hurler holds an AL record that is certain never to be broken. In a night game at Yankee Stadium on August 4, 1953, in the process of drubbing Ted Gray of the Tigers 15-0 he racked up seven RBI, the most ever by a pitcher in an AL game. We itch to give you a RBI double for his name.

6 Who was the last Yankees pitcher to sock two homers in one game? It was quite an outing as one of them was a grand slam, contributing to his six-RBI performance. Although he won just eight games that year, he bagged 20 twice in pinstripes while toiling for seven Yankees flag winners, six of whom won it all. No small potato, he's good for a RBI double.

7 On June 10, 2002, this frosh infuriated the Diamondbacks Randy Johnson by blasting a homer on the first big league pitch he ever saw, which also proved to be his only four-bagger in pinstripes. RBI single.

8 What Yankees hurler holds the AL record for the most consecutive batters retired? Over a three-game stretch he mowed down 38 straight, and finished the season with 18 victories, a league-leading .818 winning percentage, plus a World Championship ring. Single for him and a RBI for the year of his famous feat.

9 On April 14, 1967, Red Sox rookie Billy Rohr was roaring along in his big league debut, carrying a no-hitter against the Yanks with two outs in the ninth until this Bomber ended it with a single. It was the only hit Rohr yielded, but the famed spoiler's worth a double.

10 What pitcher's stick was so respected that he once served as a DH in the Yankees starting lineup and batted sixth? The Bombers staff leader with 16 wins in 1987, he added 12 more a year later, and on June 11 of that season he hit a sac fly RBI in his lone at bat on the day of his famous feat. Winner of 151 career games, he twice cracked three homers in a season while in the senior circuit. RBI single.

11 The first Yankee to hammer three homers in a game never won a loop four-bagger crown in the majors but earned one big-time in the minors. Work those clues for a RBI double.

> **AB**: 11
> **Hits**: 11
> **Total Bases**: 20
> **RBI**: 11

INNING 7
MEMORABLE MONIKERS

1 Scooter. Start off here with an easy single.

2 Poosh 'em Up. RBI single.

3 Bam-Bam. Triple.

4 Braggo. Homer for the last name of this one-time AL home run king.

5 What was Mickey Mantle's real first name? Double.

6 Chicken. RBI single.

7 Spud. RBI double.

8 Dirt. Single.

9 Stick. Single.

10 Twinkletoes. Double.

11 Louisiana Lightning. A slow rolling single.

12 Cuddles. RBI triple.

> **AB**: 12
> **Hits**: 12
> **Total Bases**: 22
> **RBI**: 5

INNING 8
FORGOTTEN UNFORGETTABLES

1 In the 44-season span between 1921 and 1964 one man—and only one man—wore Yankees garb for as long as three consecutive seasons without ever getting to cash a World Series check. He was far from a benchwarmer, working in 87 games and 413 innings in his three years as a Bomber, but it's back to the bench for aspiring experts who whiff on this potential two-run homer, plus an extra ribby for nailing this Forgotten Unforgettable's three-year stay with the Yanks.

2 Who was the first man to play 100 games in a season for the Bombers without ever playing the field? Of course he was a DH, and he did it during the first season of its deployment. Easy to skip a beat and forget here. Double.

3 The Mets collected former Yankees in droves during their early years. Who was the first performer to go the opposite route and leave the then lowly Mets to play with the Bombers? Born in the Big Apple, this Forgotten Unforgettable lefty-swinging first baseman–outfielder hit just .211 in 124 career games, six of them with the 1965 Yanks during his big league coda. Leon was his given name, but he carried the same moniker as a Dodgers great of his era. Hook slide triple.

4 Mickey Mantle's name leaps to every mind in answer to the question: Who hit the most career homers of any switch-hitting outfielder that wore Yankees livery? But we guarantee the name of the gardener whose mark the Mick eclipsed will be a forgotten figure by all but a select few experts. Three-run homer.

5 What gardener subbed a lot for an ailing Babe Ruth in 1925 and racked up a 1.028 OPS and a .360 BA in 89 games and then returned to the bench the following year where he languished for most of the remainder of his career before departing the majors in 1929? Stuck in Yankees garb in a time when free agency was only a dim concept, in his eight ML seasons our forgotten fly chaser hit a stellar .309 but had just 787 at bats. Three of them, however, came as a pinch hitter for Lou Gehrig, which is two more than any other Yankee during Lou's record consecutive-games streak can claim. Solo homer.

6 Rip a grand slam if you know the forgotten frosh lefty who joined the New York AL entry late in the 1907 campaign and tossed three shutouts in six starts to finish with a 4-2 record and a snazzy 2.17 ERA only to disappear mysteriously and forever from the scene before the bell rang to begin the 1908 season.

7 Ready for another grand slammer? Look no further than this journeyman shortstop who tagged 15 homers and hit .257 for Greensboro of the Carolina League in 1964. Given special permission to be added to the Bombers World Series roster due to an injury to Tony Kubek, he did naught but ride the wood for all seven games. In truth, he never tasted big league java in his entire pro career, before or after the 1964 Series, but he nonetheless had a Fall Classic check to cash. Chances are only a precious few will follow our slippery path here and track down this forgotten Series-eligible fill-in.

8 Pitchers who disappear forever from the bigs after making as many as 20 starts in their maiden seasons have been few and far between since expansion. Guaranteed, we'll slip this one-year unforgettable Yankees humpty who went 7-12 in 22 starts in 1991 with a wretched 6.27 ERA past just about everyone. Even after telling you that he shares the same first name as a regular third baseman on a subsequent

Bombers world champ, we'll ante up a RBI double for the flinger who helped make 1991 one of the most eminently forgettable unforgettable seasons in Yankees history.

9 The Yankees season record holder for walks issued with 179, this forgotten flinger led the AL in free passes three straight years including one season when he failed to hurl enough innings to qualify for the ERA title! Must have been on some bad teams, right? Matter of fact, he was a valued member of some of the Yankees most unforgettable clubs. RBI single.

10 A reserve outfielder with the Yanks from 1961 through 1963, he hit just one homer in 222 career games, all in pinstripes. However, he made his four-bagger count, blasting a game winning shot against the Tigers in the 22nd inning on June 24, 1962. Two-bagger for this unforgettable figure's moment in Yankees history.

11 Billy Martin was the first man to serve three separate stints at the Yankees helm in the course of taking the Yanks reins on no less than five different occasions. Do you know who was the first player to be able to claim he served as many as three separate stints in pinstripes? In addition to telling you that his three tours enabled him to play with both Joe DiMaggio and Tom Tresh, we'll note that enough clues are here for every astute reader to romp to a triple.

AB: 11
Hits: 11
Total Bases: 33
RBI: 17

INNING 9
RBI RULERS

1 Who is the oldest Yankee to plate 100 mates in a season? We think the answer will surprise many readers, so we'll go for two here, plus a RBI for the year of his elder achievement.

2 What Yankee shares the post-1920 record with Richie Ashburn for fewest RBI in a season with as many as 150 games played? Okay, he was a shortstop, but solid range and a strong arm couldn't offset his .532 OPS and 20 RBI that season. A native of Venezuela, his name's worth a single, plus a RBI for his year of ribby futility.

3 When Mickey Mantle logged 87 RBI in 1952, he set a new Yankees season record for ribbies by a switch hitter. Whose long-standing record did he break?

4 Between 1920 and 1936, either Ruth or Gehrig led the Yankees in RBI in every season but one. Collect a double by naming the only other Bomber to slip between this power-house pair, plus a RBI for the year he broke the Ruth-Gehrig chokehold.

5 When Lou Gehrig knocked home 184 mates in 1931, whose all-time record for the most RBI by a first baseman did he break? RBI double.

6 On 14 occasions, the Yanks have had a slugger knock in as many as 150 runs in a season. However, there are only three names on the list of Yankees with 150-RBI seasons. Name all three for a scratch single.

7 Who led a Yankees World Champion in RBI despite missing 38 games during the regular season? Telling you it was the first of his seven consecutive team ribby leaderships makes this one a single, but add an RBI for the year in question.

8 The 1936 Yankees featured a record five men who collected as many as 100 RBI. Four are in the Hall of Fame. Bag a double if you know the only one that isn't.

9 Who set the Yankees pre-Lively Ball era record for both the most home runs and the most RBI in a season by a pitcher when he had 20 ribbies and went deep four times in 1915? Triple.

10 Who is the only second baseman besides Tony Lazzeri to knock in 100 runs in a season more than once while wearing Yankees garb? RBI single.

AB: 10
Hits: 10
Total Bases: 16
RBI: 6

GAME 3

INNING 1
BULLPEN BLAZERS

1 Pure bullpen operatives were rare when the Yanks captured their first flag in 1921. Their staff ace that year co-led the AL in wins and paced the Bombers in starts while sharing the junior circuit lead with seven saves. Take another easy bingle.

2 Now the tough get going. What tosser topped the AL in saves, relief wins and ERA while notching 19 victories for the Murderers Row gang? RBI single.

3 He had more nicknames than he did pitches, but his most apt moniker was "Fireman." Holder prior to 1962 of the ML career record for saves, he collected all but three of his 107 saves in Yankees attire. Single.

4 Over a three-year stretch this well-traveled Yankees southpaw came out of the pen 218 times and didn't record a single save. Not even *one*? Exactly, and in parts of seven seasons in the Bronx he logged just 15 saves in over 450 outings. Take a single for naming this late-inning role player.

5 Who fanned the most batters in a season of any Yankees reliever during the 1980s? Telling you this one's good for three should steer you off the Goose.

6 A voracious appetite for nightlife shortened his career, but for five seasons, from 1945 through 1949, he was the best reliever in the game. Just a single for this lefty who held the Yankees season record for saves with 27 prior to AL expansion in 1961.

7 Who holds the Bombers record for wins in a season by a pitcher who worked less than 100 innings? In just $85\frac{1}{3}$ innings this reliever bagged 14 victories in 44 outings for a Yankees outfit that won 103 games. RBI single.

8 What former NL 20-game winner joined the Yankees in 1942 and became their top bullpenner during World War II? If we tell you that his allegiance to the Yanks didn't end there, all we can award is a bloop two-bagger.

9 Here's one you can hit for distance. Although Mariano made it habitual, who was the last Yankees closer prior to Rivera to record as many as 30 saves in a season while posting an ERA below two? Believe it or not, a triple.

10 The first AL flag to fly over New York nearly arrived in 1904. On a staff that bagged 123 complete games in 155 starts, what younger brother of a Hall of Fame hurler topped the New York ALers in relief appearances with a mere nine? Homer.

11 Who suffered the most losses in a season (11) by a Yankees bullpen operative? In the process he posted a league-leading 27 saves for a world champ and two years later racked up an AL-tying 33 more. Single for him and a RBI for the year he piled up those defeats.

   AB: 11
   Hits: 11
   Total Bases: 19
   RBI: 4

INNING 2
HOME RUN KINGS

1 The youngest Yankee to punch 30 homers in a season is also the youngest Bomber to club 40 taters, and he eclipsed both figures in the same campaign. Single for him, plus a RBI for the year of his youthful slamming.

2 What Yankee was the first rookie in World Series history to pound two homers in one game? Knowing that he victimized fellow freshman Junior Thompson for both shots still makes this one a double, plus a RBI for the year.

3 Who had the most seasons as a Yankee in which he collected as many as 400 at bats while hitting fewer than 10 homers? He did it 12 times, connecting for a career-high seven taters twice. You know he's a middle infielder, but we'll boldly wager a triple you'll guess the wrong one.

4 In 1938 five Yankees hit 20 or more homers. Three were Hall of Famers Lou Gehrig, Joe DiMaggio and Bill Dickey. Name the other two and win a double. No credit for just one.

5 What Yankee hammered 23 homers at Shea Stadium over a two-year stretch? Being told he wasn't a visitor those seasons despite sporting Bombers garb narrows this to a RBI single.

6 In the Yankees long history only one performer to date who collected as many as 2,500 plate appearances while wearing their uniform tagged less than five home runs. He left the Big Apple prior to the 1910 season with just four dingers to his credit in Yankees livery. Nonetheless he owned the top batting average, OPS and on-base percentage among all shortstops with as many as 2,000 plate appearances in the American League's first decade of existence. Kid you not, that info should be more than enough to herd you to a two-bagger.

7 When Wally Pipp set a new Yankees club record with 12 homers in 1916 in the process of leading the AL in four-baggers, what other Yankee also shattered the old club record of six by creaming 10 taters? Two-run double.

8 In 13 ML seasons this outfielder made the rounds, playing on seven different clubs. However, he made his brief stay in pinstripes memorable slamming a whopping 16 homers in just 132 at bats for a Yankees world champ before closing his ML stay with the Angels the following season. Double for this mountain of a man.

9 Who is the most recent Yankees first baseman to lead the AL in home runs? Triple, plus a RBI for the year.

10 When Lou Gehrig hit four homers in a game in 1932, what event that occurred that same day overshadowed his feat on the nation's sport pages? RBI double.

> **AB**: 10
> **Hits**: 10
> **Total Bases**: 20
> **RBI**: 7

INNING 3
MASTER MOUNDSMEN

1 Who was the first Yankee to lead the AL in pitching strikeouts? Tough enough to rate a triple, plus two RBI for the year.

2 Russ Ford set the Yankees rookie K record when he fanned 209 batters in 1910. How long would it be until another Yankees hurler struck out as many as 200 batters in a season? Solo homer.

3 Who became the only Yankees ERA qualifier in history to log a sub-2.00 ERA with less than 100 strikeouts when he posted a 1.94 ERA with 92 Ks in 1914? Two-run triple.

4 Frank Lary was known as "The Yankee Killer" because he flaunted a 28-13 career record against the Bombers. What Hall of Famer might have become the all-time "Yankee Killer" if the Bombers had not wisely short-circuited his mastery of them by trading for him after he launched his career with a dazzling 17-5 record against the team in pinstripes? RBI single.

5 Who is the only pitcher to win as many as 25 games in a season twice in a Yankees uniform? This one causes even top Bronx buffs to scratch their heads, so we're going for three bases, if you can make it.

6 What southpaw holds the post-Deadball Era season record for the most losses by a Yankee with a sub-3.00 ERA? RBI triple for a man whose W-L records during his career almost exactly mirrored the quality of the teams behind him.

7 What hurler won his 200th game in 1934 while a member of the Yankees after being paid most of his career to beat the Bombers? We'll reveal that he twice led the AL in both wins and complete games between 1922 and 1926 and also add that he labored most of his career in his hometown for a team that beat Brooklyn in its first World Series appearance and still award a RBI double.

8 In their lengthy history, the Yankees have had only six 20-game losers and none in over 40 years now. What was the only year the Yanks had two 20-game losers? Two-run homer, plus an extra RBI for each hurler you can name.

9 Who is the only Yankee since the late 1920s to work as many as 275 innings in a season while yielding fewer than 10 homers? Ground balls were the key to his game, as this lefty featured a sharp-breaking sinker for over 20 years. Single, plus a RBI for the year.

10 The Yanks have never had a pitcher win and lose 20 games in the same season. Who came the closest when he lost 19 in 1904 while winning more than 20? RBI double.

AB: 10
Hits: 10
Total Bases: 26
RBI: 13

INNING 4
NO-HIT NUGGETS

1 For many years he was credited with authoring the first Yankees no-hitter after throwing nine hitless frames against Cleveland on August 30, 1910, before losing 5-0 in 11 innings. Now the honor belongs elsewhere according to Major League Baseball's present rules even though many, including your authors, still recognize his gem as a no-no. Who is he for a three-bagger?

2 The first Yankee to throw a no-hitter during a Bomber flag-winning season had the unique experience of failing to fan a single batter when he victimized the Philadelphia A's on September 4, 1923. Who was he? Two-bagger.

3 The first hurler to toss two no-hitters in the same season for an AL team was a Yankee. His name brings a single, plus a RBI for the year he did it.

4 Who pitched a complete game no-hitter for a Yankees world champ but failed to make the club's postseason roster that year? An 11-7 slate made him look much better than he performed, as he allowed 14 runners per nine innings while posting a 5.01 ERA. Interestingly, the no-no was his only complete game for the Bombers. Single for him, plus a RBI for the year.

5 Who broke up Bill Bevens's bid to become the first hurler to author a no-hit game in World Series competition with a pinch double with two out in the ninth in Bevens's 2-1 loss to Brooklyn in the 1947 Fall Classic? Single.

6 What Hall of Fame hurler won a tense 1-0 no-hitter in Yankee Stadium against a Yankees lineup that included Joe

DiMaggio, Phil Rizzuto, Joe Gordon, Tommy Henrich, Charlie Keller and the luckless Bill Bevens? Double.

7 Who was the youngest pitcher to toss a no-no with the Bombers? Telling you that he never started another game for the Yanks after that season should lead you to a single, plus a RBI for the year.

8 Which, if any, of these Yankees Hall of Famers tossed at least one no-hitter during his career? Jack Chesbro, Herb Pennock, Waite Hoyt, Red Ruffing, Whitey Ford, Babe Ruth. Two-run single.

9 Who pitched a no-hitter against the Pinstripers after logging over 1,700 innings with the Yankees? Winner of nearly one hundred games for the Yanks during the Deadball Era, he held them hitless at Hilltop while sporting Tribe flannels on September 10, 1919. Triple.

10 What Yankee tossed a no-hitter a year after setting the club record for consecutive losses in a season with 11? The defending World Champion Red Sox went hitless against his slants on April 24, 1917, at Fenway Park. But you can mow down the answer for a homer.

11 Who fired a no-hitter for the Yanks *before* he ever threw a pitch in the minors? Debuting with another AL outfit in 1989, he didn't taste bush league ball until after he returned to his original club in 1996. His no-no is even more impressive considering what he overcame to make the majors. Single.

AB: 11
Hits: 11
Total Bases: 20
RBI: 6

INNING 5
WHAT WAS THEIR REAL HANDLE?

1 Chris Chambliss. Double.

2 Deacon McGuire. RBI triple.

3 Mickey Rivers. Triple.

4 Butch Wynegar. Triple.

5 Noodles Hahn. Home run.

6 Allie Reynolds. Triple.

7 Bernie Williams. Single.

8 Dutch Ruether. RBI triple.

9 Muddy Ruel. Triple.

10 Lefty Gomez. RBI single.

11 Tino Martinez. Single.

12 Bucky Dent. Double.

AB: 12
Hits: 12
Total Bases: 29
RBI: 4

INNING 6
CIRCLING THE GLOBE

1 The first man born outside the U.S. to swat 100 career homers smacked them all in pinstripes and hit over .300 as a regular three times. A two-time All-Star, this Canadian also played in six World Series with the Yanks, winning all but one. Two bases.

2 What switch hitter crushed 350 homers including 19 in his final season while playing on a Yankees world champ? Knowing he was the DH when David Cone tossed his perfecto against the Expos makes you a stone cold cinch to single here, but add a RBI for identifying his country of origin.

3 The Dominican Republic has proved to be fertile ground for big league talent. Can you name the first man to play for the Yanks who was born there? Debuting in 1963, he would go on to appear at first, second, short and in the outfield with the Bombers. After he compiled 101 games and a .266 average, the Yanks dealt him during the 1965 season to the Tribe, where he played more regularly before bowing out two years later. Two-run double.

4 The Yankees have had many great players of Italian descent, led by Joe DiMaggio, Yogi Berra and Phil Rizzuto. However, they've had just one player in their long history that was born in Italy. Treat yourself, literally, to a rugged three-run homer if you can name this PCL mainstay who hurled two innings for the Bombers on April 30, 1947, before being shipped back to the minors.

5 For years John Anderson held the record for the most at bats in a New York AL uniform by a player born in Norway. What backstop broke his mark of 657 ABs in 1936 before receiving his second of what would eventually be five World Series checks? Solo homer.

6 Most teams with roots in the 19th century have a Hall of Famer or two that was born in Ireland. The Yankees' best-known Ireland-born performer was this Belfast native who appeared in 48 games with the New Yorkers in 1908 and 1909. His real name was Henry, but they called him "Irish" and call yourself the lucky winner of a grand slam if you know him.

7 Which Yankee is the only big leaguer to date ever born in China? Son of a Congregationalist missionary, his career lasted all of four games as a first baseman–pinch hitter in 1914. Off the field, he made a far greater impact, returning to China as a missionary and physical education teacher. Later he served as General Secretary of Stiles Hall at Berkeley, and subsequently lobbied actively for civil rights. Even adding that he shares a surname with a two-time NL homer champ who briefly played in pinstripes still makes this man worth a seat-reacher with the sacks full.

8 Born in Wales, he gave the Yankees two full years of duty at third base in 1909 and 1910 before moving to the St. Louis Browns, where he finished his career in 1929 at the age of 49. Telling you that he once held the Yankees record for the most career switch hits may help nail down this three-bagger.

9 In 1998 this gawky 6' 7" lefty posted a 1.67 ERA in 50 games from the pen. Two years earlier he had made four appearances during the 1996 Series and earned his first win with the Bombers in Game 4 in relief of Mariano Rivera. All told, this Aussie worked 109 regular season games across parts of three campaigns in pinstripes, and he's good for a clean single.

10 Taiwanese-born Yankee Chien Ming-Wang tied Johan Santana for the big league lead in wins in 2006 and in the process set a new single-season record for victories by an

Asian-born pitcher, besting South Koran Chan Ho Park, who won 18 in 2000. Whose Yankees club record did Wang break for the most wins by an Asian-born pitcher? Two bagger.

11 Though he was far from the first Cuban-born performer to play for the Yankees, he was the first to cash a World Series check signed by George Weiss. He received it in 1953 after coming to the Yanks from the St. Louis Browns and seemed the following year to be the heir apparent to Phil Rizzuto's job before being dealt to Baltimore, where he spent his last five seasons in the show. Worth a triple.

12 Oh, how those Yankees scouts loved his power, and during his days in the bushes he showed them why, creaming over 20 homers six times. Up top, it was a different story for this Curacao clubber as he poked a mere 12 four-baggers across 159 games, bouncing up and down between the Yanks and their farm system from 1989 through 1993. Double.

AB: 12
Hits: 12
Total Bases: 32
RBI: 15

INNING 7
STELLAR STICKWIELDERS

1 Who holds the Yankees club record for the highest batting average in a season with 400 or more at bats? After learning that he failed to win the AL batting crown, in his record-setting season, you're a heavy favorite to collect a double for the player, plus an extra base if you know who beat him out for the bat title.

2 In 1941 Joe DiMaggio hit .357, but that was the year Ted Williams chose to hit .406. Who is the only Yankee since 1941 to hit .350 or better and fail to win the AL batting title? Single for him, extra base for both the year and the man who beat him out.

3 Who posted the most total bases in a season by a Yankee whose name isn't Ruth, Gehrig or DiMaggio? We'll wager a double that you'll whiff here, plus a RBI for the year he racked up the sacks.

4 The Yankees have never had a .400 hitter. Amazingly, they have never even had a *part-time* .400 hitter. The team record for the most at bats in a season with an average of .400 or above belongs to a career .263 stick that hit .405 in a season that was shortened by military service obligations to just 11 games and 42 at bats. Can you nail him for a two-run homer?

5 Who was the first Bomber in the expansion era to top the AL in runs scored for two straight seasons? For the first of his Yankees leaderships, he posted the highest total in the junior loop in 36 years and crossed the plate a combined 276 times over the two campaigns. Single.

6 A few moments of careful thought should tell you who has logged the highest season slugging average to date in pinstripes of any player eligible for the Hall of Fame who has not yet made it. RBI single.

7 No Yankees slugger has ever enjoyed a season in which he clocked as many as 20 triples in combination with 30 or more home runs. Who came the closest to date by legging out 18 triples to go with a 30+ homer season? RBI single, plus an extra base for the year.

8 When Babe Ruth collected 388 total bases in his first year as a Yankee, he shattered the previous club record by a margin of 121. Who held the old club season record with 267 total bases? Two-run homer for him and a RBI for his big year.

9 How's this for a model of consistency? Who posted these exact same totals for two consecutive Yankees flag-winners: 17 homers, 6 triples and 32 doubles? A steady performer, he quietly went about his business while his more boisterous mates made headlines. Three-bagger.

10 In 1961 Roger Maris set the current Yankees record for the most total bases (366) with a sub-.300 batting average. A two-run triple says you don't know who held the record prior to Maris.

11 Whose Yankees club career record for the most hits by a switch hitter did Mickey Mantle break when he garnered his 637th hit in 1955? Solo homer for this toughie.

    AB: 11
    Hits: 11
    Total Bases: 28
    RBI: 12

INNING 8
RBI RULERS

1 Two men, with 22 apiece, hold the Yankees club record for the most RBI in a season by a pitcher. One is Red Ruffing who did it twice. Who is the other? Solo homer, plus two RBI for the year.

2 Who held the pre-divisional era season record for the most RBI by a Yankees third baseman? RBI double, plus an extra base for his record-setting season.

3 Who posted the most 100 RBI seasons among Yankees switch hitters? RBI single.

4 Two Yanks have driven in 100 runs in a season while collecting as many as 150 singles. Both achieved this feat since World War II and their seasons came 11 years apart. One base apiece and a RBI for each year.

5 Who drew the fewest walks by any Yankees 100-RBI man? In so doing, he broke Bobby Richardson's club record for at bats in a season by totaling 696, while coaxing just 23 free passes to go with 102 RBI. Single for him, plus a RBI for the year.

6 Joe DiMaggio drove in 100 runs in each of his first seven seasons up top. Only one other Yankee did so in as many as his first three campaigns. He's a RBI single.

7 What Yankee averaged an AL-best 103 RBI per season during the three war years, 1943–1945? RBI single.

8 Whose record for the most career RBI in Yankees garb did Babe Ruth break in 1926 when he notched his 826th ribby as a Bomber? RBI single.

9 What Hall of Famer set a still-existing Yankees record for the fewest RBI by a regular outfielder when he could knock home just 17 mates in 1907? The Hall of Fame clue makes this worth only a double.

10 Who is the only Yankee to date to drive in 100 runs in a season in which he'd have failed to qualify for the batting crown under today's rules? His 472 plate appearances would have left him 30 shy when he posted the first of his four consecutive 100 RBI seasons. Double for him and a RBI for the year.

11 The Yankees record for the most RBI in a season with less than 10 home runs is 121. Who holds it? RBI single.

> **AB**: 11
> **Hits**: 11
> **Total Bases**: 17
> **RBI**: 12

INNING 9
RED-HOT ROOKIES

1 What position did Joe DiMaggio play in his rookie season? Single.

2 In 1947 a certain rookie hurler was called up from the Yanks Newark farm team in the heat of the pennant race and played a major role in the Bombers winning the flag when he went 7-2. We'll add that he finished his career with a stupendous 120-49 won-lost record in pinstripes and award a RBI single for this 1947 rookie flash.

3 What gardener set the mark for the highest on-base percentage by a Yankees rookie according to batting title rules then in effect despite collecting less than 400 at bats in his frosh season? Your clue is he totaled nearly 500 plate appearances that year for a Yankees World Champion. Triple.

4 Knowing the Yanks most recent rookie 20-game winner can earn you a double, plus a RBI for the year he did it.

5 Joe DiMaggio placed eighth in the MVP voting as a rookie in 1936, the highest finish by a Yankees frosh prior to World War II. What Bombers yearling topped DiMaggio when he finished a strong fourth in the AL MVP race in 1943? Tough triple for some but routine for our experts.

6 Who was the most recent Yankees rookie to win a starting assignment in a World Series game? He went 12-4 during the regular season with a 3.13 ERA and bagged Game 2 of a Series sweep. The books list him as being 33 at the time, but many suspect he was older. Single.

7 This southpaw paced AL freshmen in ERA, starts, innings, complete games and losses and tied for the top spot in victories. Blanked in that year's Rookie of the Year balloting, he won 20 games in pinstripes four seasons later. Double, plus a RBI for his frosh campaign.

8 The man who hit .314 and won Rookie of the Year honors on the first Yankees team in 18 years to call themselves world champs is an infield single.

9 When Joe DiMaggio clubbed 29 homers in 1936 to set the Yanks current record for the most dingers by a rookie, whose old mark did he break? Single, plus a RBI for the year the old standard was set.

10 What Yankees rookie pitched his first complete game in the bigs in a World Series? Just 6-9 in 128 innings during the regular season, he started Game 5 in 1978 and defeated the Dodgers 12-2 in the only Fall Classic appearance of his nine-year career. Double.

AB: 10
Hits: 10
Total Bases: 17
RBI: 3

GAME 4

INNING 1
JACK OF ALL TRADES

1 What regular outfielder on two Yankees pennant winners later won three Gold Gloves in pinstripes at another position? He might have earned even more had he not switched places with a certain aging Bomber and returned to the outfield after winning the first two. Double, plus an extra base for the man whose failing legs necessitated the switch.

2 He broke in with the Yanks as a shortstop. After serving as the Bombers regular third sacker in his first full season in the bigs, he moved the following year and was the second baseman on each of the Yankees first three flag winners. Award yourself a triple.

3 His primary position was third base the season he was voted the AL Rookie of the Year, but he played shortstop the season his line drive through the box short-circuited Herb Score's career and second base the only year the Yanks lost to a Brooklyn team in the World Series. Name the San Francisco native who spent his entire 10-year career in pinstripes. Single.

4 How about a four-time All-Star who swiftly declined in every phase of his game after turning 31? A Gold Glove infielder prior to donning pinstripes, he inexplicably lost the ability to throw to first, forcing a switch to the outfield in 2001. Single.

5 Born in Golden, Colorado, he played third base for the Yankees in 1911 after coming to the club from the St. Louis Browns. Two years later he saw duty mostly at second base for the New Yorkers and then wrapped up his 11-year career by returning to the outfield, where he spent the majority of his time in the majors. He retired in 1916 with the most hits at that juncture of any Yankee during the decade of the 1910s. Three-run homer even after we clue you that his last name is pronounced the same as that of a gardener that led the AL in walks five times in the first decade of the 20th century.

6 The "M&M Boys" dominated the Yankees outfield in 1961. A single comes your way for naming the All-Star performer earlier in his career at another position who placed third that year in games played in the Bombers pasture with 87.

7 What Yankees jack-of-all-trades saw duty at first base, third base, catcher and the outfield in World Series action? Learning that in his first Series he started one game in left field while Enos Slaughter started the other six should guide you to a two-bagger, plus a RBI for knowing his first Series appearance.

8 A two-run homer is yours if you know the Yankees Handy-Andy infielder in the 1930s that broke in as a second baseman in 1932, was the Bombers semi-regular third baseman in 1934, and played the most innings at first base between 1926 and 1938 of any Yankee that was not named Lou Gehrig. Those ancients who recall the 1934 affair when Joe McCarthy penciled an ailing Gehrig into the lineup at shortstop so Lou could get one at bat in the top of the first inning and thus extend his consecutive game streak should also recall that our man played that entire game at the initial cushion.

9 After serving as the Pirates regular shortstop in 1902, he jumped to the first AL team to represent the city of New York the following year and was immediately moved to third base. Later in his tour with the Yankees he occupied left field for two seasons on a regular basis and also saw spot duty at second and first base. When he left the club prior to the 1909 season to go to Washington, he stood second only to Willie Keeler in career hits as a Yankee. Solo homer for the man whose real first name was William but was best known by a nickname that rhymes with the moniker of the leader in career games played at second base prior to 1901.

10 Switched from the pasture to first base after the infamous acquisition of free agent disaster Steve Kemp, he adjusted and hit a team-leading .306. At one point in his career he served as a regular outfielder with a club who defeated the Yanks in the Series. RBI single, plus an extra base for the year he shifted positions.

11 Only two men have hurled as many as 30 career innings in Yankees garb and also logged a 100-RBI season for the Bombers. One is easy, the other elevates this question to a two-run homer if you nail both.

12 What Yankees fumbler somehow won a Gold Glove in the outfield after beginning his career as a regular at another position? Despite knowing that he was miscue prone, the Yanks later returned him to the position they knew he couldn't play and he rewarded their acumen by committing more errors in one season than any other Bomber since World War II, regardless of position. Double for him, plus an extra base for pegging his original defensive spot.

AB: 12
Hits: 12
Total Bases: 32
RBI: 10

INNING 2
HOME RUN KINGS

1 What Hall of Famer pounded a homer both for and against the Yanks in a Fall Classic and in so doing became the first player in history to drill Series' taters in both leagues? RBI single.

2 Who posted the lowest OBP by a Yankee who belted as many as 30 homers in a season? Although he popped a team-leading 31 dingers, he drew just 29 walks in 585 at bats, and six were intentional. A Brooklyn-born Bomber, he's good for a single, plus a RBI for the year of his .290 OBP.

3 Before Bernie Williams cracked 29 homers to top the 1996 Yanks, who had been the last Yankees switch hitter to swat as many as 25 dingers in a season? After clouting a team-leading 26 bombs, he followed with 27 more before his numbers sharply plummeted. RBI single.

4 Who was the first man to club as many as 20 career home runs in a New York AL uniform? Surprise yourself and nail a triple.

5 In the final AL season prior to expansion, Roger Maris lost the junior circuit home run crown to Mickey Mantle by a margin of just one dinger—40 to 39. What slugger finished third that year in the AL dinger race with 38, just two behind Mantle? Two-run homer.

6 Gehrig, DiMaggio and Berra had years when their homers exceeded their strikeout totals. Since expansion, no Yankee who clubbed as many as 20 homers in a season has accomplished this feat. However, a certain lefty-swinging first baseman–DH one year pounded 23 taters in 295 at bats for the Bombers while fanning just 25 times. Two bases and two RBI for the year.

7 In DiMag's final season of 1951 he hit just 12 homers. Who led the club with 27 and also topped them in RBI with 88? Only rates a single.

8 In 1946 when all the Yankees pre-war stars returned to action from military service, which of them led the club in homers with 30? Two-bagger.

9 Besides Roger Maris, what other Minnesota native flashed exceptional power for the 1961 outfit but as a part-timer as he poled 21 homers in just 243 at bats, including a team-record four pinch blasts? Double.

10 What Yankee is the only player in big league history to club 40 homers in a season twice without driving in 100 runs? Scratch hit, plus a RBI for each year.

AB: 10
Hits: 10
Total Bases: 18
RBI: 9

INNING 3
TUMULTUOUS TRADES

Today the Yankees rely heavily on the free-agent market to reload at positions where they have holes, but earlier Bombers editions took ruthless advantage of other AL clubs in desperate need of cash and/or warm bodies. The Yanks have not always come out on the long end of the stick in deals, however. Can you identify the stars that both came to and left the Bronx via the trade route in the following one-sided transactions?

1 The present-day Yankees launched their first season as part of the American League with ex-Boston NL star Herman Long at shortstop and a utilityman named Ernie Courtney, who later became a marginal third baseman with the Phillies. On June 10, 1903, they swapped both Long and Courtney to Detroit for what fiery early-day Gotham star shortstop? Homer.

2 The swindle the Yankees engineered against the Red Sox on March 22, 1972, is so notorious that we're offering you only a single for naming *both* players in this straight-up swap. Nothing for less.

3 In 18 seasons he stroked over 2,200 hits, won two batting crowns and stole more than 350 bases. Alas, none of that was achieved in pinstripes because the Yankees management just had to get their hands on lefty Bob Sykes, who never again pitched in the majors. A double for the star that got away.

4 While working as Cleveland's General Manager, Gabe Paul pulled a double whammy on the Tribe that has never been fully investigated. On November 27, 1972, he packaged a future Yankees star and Gerry Moses to the Bronx in exchange for Charlie Spikes, plus three others to sweeten the deal. Then, scarcely six weeks later, Paul jumped ship and joined the Yankees front office. Single for the player Gabe fiddled from Cleveland for his future employer.

5 In the early 1920s the woeful Red Sox were the equivalent of the Kansas City A's franchise in the late 1950s in that they provided the Yankees with a constant stream of useful players in return for hordes of has-beens and mediocrities. What Hall of Fame hurler did the Yankees plunder from the Sox on January 30, 1923, in exchange for Camp Skinner, Norm McMillan, George Murray and $50,000? Double.

6 Pitcher Ken Wright and what outfielder–DH who would spend over a decade in pinstripes came in exchange for fast-fading 38-year-old reliever Lindy McDaniel? Single for this temperamental Tampa native.

7 When Joe Gordon, the Yankees star pre-war second sacker, returned from military duty in 1946 and hit just .210, the Bombers thought he was over the hill and dealt him to Cleveland. Gordon proved he still had something left in the tank and helped the Tribe win the 1948 pennant, but the player Cleveland furnished the New Yorkers in exchange for Gordon and third baseman Eddie Bockman starred in six World Series while in pinstripes. Who was he? Just a single.

8 Who went on to hit the most career homers after the Bombers sent him packing? Look no further than this Kentucky clubber, who slammed over 300 taters elsewhere, including three straight seasons of as many as 40. Who did the Yanks receive in return for him? Only journeyman Ken Phelps. Cringe your way to a single.

9 In a gigantic two-part 18-player trade with Baltimore in the fall of 1954, what two future World Series pitching stars did the Yankees acquire from the Baltimore Orioles? We'll clue you that the pair were a combined 17-36 with the 1954

Orioles and that one led the AL in losses and the other in walks and still give a triple for both. No credit for only one.

10 The Yankees long coveted Kansas City A's star Hector Lopez before finally swinging a deal for him on May 26, 1959, that gave the A's Jerry Lumpe, Tom Sturdivant and Johnny Kucks. What former Yankees hurler and future 20-game winner returned to the Bombers along with Lopez in the KC raid—er, trade? Two-run double.

11 This one's not so easy. On December 11, 1935, the Yankees swapped temperamental Johnny Allen to Cleveland, only to see him win 20 games for the Tribe in 1936 and then lead the AL in winning percentage in 1937. But Yankees GM Ed Barrow had nothing to regret because in return for Allen the Yanks garnered Steve Sundra, who would post a snazzy 11-1 record with the 1939 Bombers, and a righthander who topped the AL in winning percentage in 1936 and followed by beating Carl Hubbell in Game 4 of the 1936 World Series. Who was he? Solo homer.

12 Arguably the worst swap in Yankees history is one even diehard Bombers fans tend to forget when the subject arises. Because this Floridian was blocked at first base by Don Mattingly, the Yanks decided to package him in a trade with the Blue Jays for a fading Dale Murray, and a minor league nobody. Just a single for him, but it's a crime if you miss this dog of a deal.

> **AB**: 12
> **Hits**: 12
> **Total Bases**: 23
> **RBI**: 4

INNING 4
WHAT WAS THEIR REAL HANDLE?

1 Goose Gossage. Single.

2 Snuffy Stirnweiss. RBI single.

3 Bud Metheny. Two-run homer.

4 Roger Clemens. Surprise double.

5 Yogi Berra. Single, but a chorus of groans if we slip this fat one by you.

6 Doc Medich. Double.

7 Slim Love. Three-run homer.

8 Catfish Hunter. Single.

9 Whitey Witt. Homer.

10 Babe Dahlgren. Three-run triple.

11 Sparky Lyle. RBI single.

12 Bud Daley. Triple.

AB: 12
Hits: 12
Total Bases: 27
RBI: 11

INNING 5
MVP MARVELS

1 The first MVP award in history came in 1911 when a Chalmers automobile was presented to the honoree in each league. The Yankees highest finisher that year was also the team's top hitter and tied with Tris Speaker for sixth place in the AL balloting. Name him for a solo homer.

2 Beginning in 1922 each league awarded a trophy to the MVP selected by eight baseball writers, one from each of the eight league cities. What Yankee finished fourth in the 1922 AL balloting? Three-bagger.

3 Babe Ruth easily won the 1923 MVP trophy to become the first Yankee so honored. But the rules for the league awards eliminated a player from further consideration once he gained the honor. As a result, what Bomber received the most MVP votes the year the Babe hit 60 home runs and would otherwise have been a lock to win the top prize? Just a single.

4 What Yankee holds the AL record for the fewest hits by a position player during a MVP season? He bested a Hall of Famer who outhit him by 25 points, drove in 16 more runs and whose OPS was 20 points higher. Single for the Bomber, RBI for the year, plus an extra base for the Cooperstown inductee who placed second in the voting.

5 The present MVP award system was introduced in 1931. Who was the first Yankee to win the top prize under the current system? Single for him, RBI for the year.

6 Who is the only man to win a MVP with the Yankees after copping one earlier with another AL team? Single for him, plus an extra base for the other club with whom he grabbed top honors.

7 Who was the first Bomber to earn MVP votes as a rookie? Yep, Joltin' Joe did it, but even after telling you someone else beat him to the punch, we'll still offer a triple for this yearling, plus a RBI for the year.

8 The lone Yankee to crack the top ten in the 1974 AL MVP voting hit .303 and possessed one of the game's strongest throwing arms before knee surgery ruined his chances of fully blossoming. Not much power in his stick, this New Jersey product closed with just 18 homers in 2,843 at bats. Few New York fans know him as the first player to stroke 100 hit seasons with the Yankees and the Mets. RBI double.

9 In 1945, despite leading the AL in batting and steals, Yankees second sacker Snuffy Stirnweiss finished only third in the MVP vote. What second baseman on a rival AL team beat him out, capturing second place behind MVP winner Hal Newhouser? Solo homer.

10 Speed counts here. If you need longer than 20 seconds to answer this one, you're on your honor to give yourself a goose egg. Prior to expansion in 1961, at least one Yankee at every position except two had been selected for a BBWAA MVP Award. Hone in swiftly on both MVP-less positions and win a RBI double.

11 The Yankees were the first team to win a pennant without having a single player crack the top ten in the MVP balloting at season's end. Their highest MVP finisher the year in question would have led the Yanks in batting at .340 but missed qualifying by 85 plate appearances. RBI double, plus an extra base for the year.

AB: 11
Hits: 11
Total Bases: 26
RBI: 8

INNING 6
MOMENTS TO REMEMBER

1 What Hall of Famer faced the Bombers in two World Series and not only batted a lofty .417 against Yankees pitching in the second clash but also gave himself not just one but *two* moments baseball will always remember when he beat the Pinstripers twice in a three-day span with game-winning homers? RBI double.

2 The plate umpire was Cy Rigler, the Giants catcher and pitcher were Pancho Snyder and Phil Douglas, and now all you need is the name of the Yankee who brazenly stole home in the fifth inning of the Yankees very first World Series game. His theft was the first of its kind by an ALer since Ty Cobb had victimized the Pirates in the 1909 World Series, and he was playing third base that day because Home Run Baker was not feeling up to snuff. Nail this career bench-warmer that gave the nation a Moment to Remember on October 5, 1921, and claim a three-run homer.

3 What Yankee played in both David Wells's and David Cone's perfect games, plus in yet a third perfecto with a different club earlier in his career? Few know he's the only man to play on the winning side in three such masterpieces. Identify him for a double and take an extra bag for naming the non-Yankees perfect game pitcher who gave him his first of three Moments to Remember.

4 The name of the Bombers hurler that helped inaugurate Yankee Stadium by beating Boston's Howard Ehmke 4-1 on Opening Day in 1923 rates a RBI double even after we clue you that he broke in with the 1913 Philadelphia A's.

5 What Hall of Fame hurler started both the soon-to-be-Yankees New York Highlanders first game ever at Washington on April 22, 1903, and the Gothamites first home game on April 30, 1903? We'll offer the hint that he had fewer career wins than another Hall of Fame hurler the Highlanders featured in their inaugural season and award a RBI single, plus an extra base for the other Cooperstown chucker.

6 Who is the only man to date to be in the starting lineup for the Yankees on an Opening Day before he celebrated his 20th birthday? The only clue you should need to double here is that he faced Boston's Bill Wight in his first ML at bat on that day to remember.

7 What Yankees catcher had a most ironic Day to Remember when he became the first player in AL history to blast three homers in the first game of a doubleheader and then ride the bench in the second contest? RBI double.

8 The most recent pitcher to slap five hits in a major league game was what Yankees rookie who would retire with more career complete games than anyone other than Whitey Ford who played exclusively in pinstripes? RBI single.

9 His career was shortened by a misdiagnosed neck ailment leaving him with scant few Moments to Remember after he became the first Yankees rookie to start Game 1 of a World Series. Once we tell you that he not only won it but he also bagged Game 5 and started Game 7, which the Yankees came back to win after he was removed in the second inning, we can only award a RBI double.

10 Upon the resumption of the infamous Pine Tar Game in 1983, Yankees skipper Billy Martin showed his disdain by fielding a lineup that had several Bombers playing out of position. Which four-time Yankees All-Star selection did Billy snidely insert in center field? Double.

11 Who was the only Bomber to collect a hit at Yankee Stadium and Shea Stadium on the same day? No, that isn't a misprint. On July 8, 2000, the Yanks and Mets played a doubleheader, switching parks between games. Name the Yankees primary leadoff batter that year who struck a single and a homer to etch his name in the oddity record books. Double.

AB: 11
Hits: 11
Total Bases: 24
RBI: 9

INNING 7
PEERLESS PILOTS

1 Who won over 100 games in his only season as Yankees skipper? Although the Bombers didn't make the Series that year, he later guided another club to a World Championship that same decade. A single plus a RBI for the year.

2 Quick now, who grabbed the Yanks reins on two occasions 20 years apart? Bunt single.

3 Playing .600+ ball and keeping your team in the pennant race until the last weekend of the season usually assures a manager of retaining his job. What Yankees pilot was fired despite doing exactly that? We'll also note that he notched 191 wins and a World Championship in his two years at the Yankees helm. RBI single, plus an extra base for the year he was canned.

4 What Bomber helmsman went 14-7 on the hill for the 1951 Brooklyn Dodgers? Just one of the many malleable bodies shoved into the job by Steinbrenner, he replaced Gene Michael during the 1982 campaign. RBI single.

5 Who is the only Yankees pilot to lead his own team's pitching staff in lowest ERA by a qualifier? Double for him, extra base for the year.

6 Who skippered the Yankees the year that Jimmy Austin was the team's rookie starting third baseman as well as much of the season that Russ Ford set most of the team's rookie pitching records? RBI double.

7 Babe Ruth desperately wanted an opportunity to manage the Yankees but never got it. Would Lou Gehrig have fared better had he lived? We'll never know. Who is the only

Hall of Fame first sacker to date to pilot the Yankees? Two-bagger.

8 What Yankees manager had the pleasure of beating the team he had formerly piloted to a NL pennant in his first World Series experience in pinstripes? Single for him and a RBI for the year.

9 Two-run homer if you can nail the lone Yankees player-manager to accomplish the Ruthian feat of leading his club in home runs.

10 Who is the only Yankees skipper to guide the Bombers to as many as 100 wins for three straight seasons? In none of those years did they win it all, and they advanced to the Series just once. Single for the skipper, plus a RBI for his three-year run.

11 Two men named Carl who never played in the majors managed the Yankees for at least one full season in the same decade. As you may have guessed, neither man went by his given name so we're offering a triple for both, but just a sac hit for one.

12 Besides Casey Stengel, who is the only other man to play against the Bombers in a World Series and then later manage them? Knowing he never saw the inside of Yankee Stadium during his stint at their helm makes this a scratch single.

AB: 12
Hits: 12
Total Bases: 22
RBI: 8

INNING 8
RED-HOT ROOKIES

1 The Yankees were among the last major league teams to integrate. In 1956 Elston Howard became the Yankees first African-American rookie as well as the team's first African-American performer. For a three-run homer who was the second African-American freshman to wear pinstripes?

2 Phil Rizzuto's original keystone partner in his rookie year was also a yearling who was so highly regarded that he temporarily displaced All-Star Joe Gordon, forcing Gordon to move to first base until the rook demonstrated that he wasn't ready yet to handle big league pitching. Who was this vaunted Yankees frosh second sacker in 1941? Triple.

3 In his first season in the bigs a certain Yankee broke the all-time rookie record for games played and finished just one RBI behind the team leader. The first clue alone should guide you to a clean single, but you can pad your stats with a RBI for the year.

4 Picked first by the Yanks during the initial free-agent draft in 1965, this hurler went 6-8 and set a team freshman record for walks with 102 in 1969. After brief looks in each of the next two seasons, the pride of Dickeyville, Wisconsin, was done. Bases-clearing triple.

5 When this lefty went 13-5 on a Yankees pennant-winner, he fanned 171 batters and posted a 2.56 ERA, the lowest qualifying figure for a Bomber rookie in 20 years. In that year's Series, he lost his Game 2 start. Two-bagger.

6 What rookie infielder on a Yankees World Championship team many years later opposed Mickey Mantle in the Fall Classic that followed the Mick's rookie season? RBI single.

7 Who set the Yankees rookie record with 43 steals while pacing AL freshman with 18 homers, 73 RBI and a league frosh-tying 34 doubles? Despite playing for a Bombers flag-winner, he was blown away in that year's rookie balloting, finishing a distant third. Single, plus a RBI for the year of his yearling effort.

8 Since George Steinbrenner's arrival, few Yankees rookies get a chance to work enough innings to qualify for the ERA title, but this hurler was among the rare exceptions, topping AL frosh in victories (12) and strikeouts (114) in 175 innings before winning 21 the following year. Single.

9 Without any fanfare whatsoever in 1954, a certain rookie set the Yankees season record for the most total bases with less than 250 plate appearances when he parlayed his nine triples in just 237 PAs into 124 total bases and a cool .340 BA. We're betting a solo homer that even plenty of our older fans in the crowd have forgotten this rook's feat.

10 What rookie nearly a century ago set the Yankees season record for the most losses by a hurler? Put this one in the drink for a two-run homer.

AB: 10
Hits: 10
Total Bases: 23
RBI: 12

INNING 9
FALL CLASSICS

1 What Yankees hurler registered a perfect 0.00 ERA in three starts and 27 innings in the 1921 World Series but nevertheless collected a loss in what proved to be the deciding eighth game when a teammate's error gave the Giants the game's only run? He's in the Hall, but you'll be kept waiting forever for enshrinement if you miss singling here.

2 Which Yankee was the first man to bat as a DH in the Fall Classic? In 11 seasons with the Bombers, he played on four pennant winners and rapped .295 in over 1,000 games in pinstripes. Yankees fans loved to chant his first name as he stepped to the plate. Just a single.

3 The Yanks perpetrated World Series sweeps in three straight fall appearances—1927, 1928 and 1932. Who was the only hurler to collect a win in each of the three Bombers blowouts? RBI double.

4 In their four-game sweep in 1928, the Yanks rattled Cardinals pitchers for nine home runs, seven by Ruth and Gehrig and one off the bat of Bob Meusel. What Yankees utility outfielder and former St. Louis Brown joined the banger brigade in Game 4 when the Bombers hit five dingers, a single-game Series record that has since been tied? Two-run triple.

5 Watch yourself here because this one's tougher than it looks. Who led Yankees regulars in batting in the 1996 Series when they won it all for the first time in 18 years? If you glove this hotshot cleanly, award yourself a two-run double.

6 You surely know both the Hall of Fame hurler that came on for the Cardinals in relief in Game 7 of the 1926 World Series and the Yankees Hall of Famer he fanned with the bases loaded and two out in the bottom of the seventh frame to save a 3-2 win for St. Louis. But do you also know both the Hall of Fame starters that got the win and the loss in that game? You need all four for a triple; single for three and a goose egg for less.

7 The first player to poke a pinch homer in the World Series was a 22-year-old rookie who connected against Brooklyn in Game 2 in 1947. A clean single for those who know their Fall Classic history.

8 What rookie starting pitcher in Game 4 of the 1932 World Series failed to survive the first inning in his lone fall appearance with the Yankees when the Cubs posted four quick runs off his righty slants? We'll clue you that he led the AL in winning percentage as a frosh and later topped it again as a member of the Tribe. RBI triple.

9 The most recent Yankee to toss a complete-game shutout in a Fall Classic did so in the deciding seventh game, bagging his second win after losing his first Series start that year to a whitewashing. His 1.80 ERA in 25 innings earned him the Series MVP, and his name will earn you a double, plus a RBI for the year of his feat.

10 The name of the Yankees controversial left fielder that led all hitters in the 1936 World Series with eight runs scored and a .455 BA is worth a homer even with the clue that he committed suicide some 12 years later in a Washington D.C. police station while in custody.

11 Two Yankees have fanned as many as ten batters twice in World Series play. The feats occurred across four different Series against four different clubs. One did it twice with Casey's crew while the other turned the trick under Joe Torre. Triple for both, a single for just one.

AB: 11
Hits: 11
Total Bases: 25
RBI: 7

GAME 5

INNING 1
ALL IN THE FAMILY

1 Name the grandfather who led the AL in RBI nearly 50 years before his grandson performed a heroic deed to ice a pennant for the Yankees. Just a single.

2 Several members of the 1936 Yankees world champs had brothers who also played in the majors. Name the only one who had a brother that played the same position he did and win a two-run double.

3 The Yankees first flag winner in 1921 featured no less than five former or future AL home run leaders. Knowing all five will bring you a triple (a single if you know as many as four), and three RBI are yours too if you know the only one of the five that had a sibling that debuted in the majors the same year the American League first placed a team in New York.

4 Who drove in 93 runs on a Yankees World Champion 17 years after his father caught 150 games for the White Sox? The family name brings a double, plus a RBI for both first names.

5 A rugged three-run homer is credited to your name if you know the Yankees outfielder during the 1908–1911 span whose younger brother epitomized the 1906 Hitless Wonders in that he hit just .075 in a 13-game trial that year with the White Sox.

6 Just once did the Yankees feature two brothers on the same pitching staff, and their combined age at the time was 86! Enough there to double for both, nada for one.

7 On September 14, 1974, the elder sibling homered for the Yanks in the first inning while his younger half connected in the sixth frame for Detroit. Baby bro retired with just 16 round-trippers, while the elder's highest seasonal figure is more than double his sibling's *career* total. Single for the family name, plus a RBI for knowing the younger brother's first name.

8 Blink and you missed his Yankees pinch-hit appearance (a strikeout) in Game 4 of the 2000 Series. By then, a relic of his former self, this controversial slugger once teamed with his twin brother on another AL flag winner. The family name's a single, plus a RBI for his lesser-known sibling's first name.

9 Try this Senior-Junior combo, with extras to boot. A certain veteran NL outfielder closed his career with the Yankees at age 40, retiring with 2,251 hits. Earlier, he briefly teamed with his two brothers and later fathered a son who belted 34 homers one year for the Blue Jays. A true family affair, you'll earn a single for the last name and a RBI for each of their first names.

10 Ready for a trio? A year after the eldest brother started 14 games for the Yanks, his sib joined the Bombers and became the first Yankees righty in 37 years to whiff 200 batters in a season. Their ace that year, he also topped them in wins (13) and ERA (2.87). The third and youngest bro won in the double figures in each of his first three seasons in the NL before his numbers sharply plummeted. Single for the family name, plus one base for each brother's first name.

11 Who were the first father and son in ML history each to fan as many as 100 times in a season? Papa popped 20 homers with a NL-leading 114 whiffs, and sonny later registered 100 Ks twice, with the second time coming in pinstripes when he powered 20 taters while playing the same position as his dad. Double.

> **AB**: 11
> **Hits**: 11
> **Total Bases**: 20
> **RBI**: 19

INNING 2
RBI RULERS

1 Only one Yankee prior to expansion managed to collect as many as 50 RBI in a season in which he hit no triples. His record RBI total actually was 72, and even more remarkably his 72 ribbies came in just 274 ABs. Who was this three-baggerless ribby king? Double.

2 Who led the Yanks in RBI five times with totals less than 100? While in pinstripes he plated 687 runs and his high of 96 was good enough for third the season the AL hit just .239. Sounds like it could be a Deadball performer, but he was born more than a quarter century after that era ended. Double.

3 The all-time record for the most RBI in two consecutive games was set by what Yankee when he knocked home 15 mates on May 23 (second game) and May 24, 1936, at Shibe Park? We'll add the clue that two years later he also played at Shibe Park but this time wearing a National League uniform and still credit a single.

4 Who was the only player to lead the Yanks in RBI while serving as their regular shortstop? Learning that he totaled just 51 ribbies and owned a .223 BA and a .284 SA tells you this happened before Ruth arrived. Homer, plus an extra RBI for the year.

5 In 1952 what Yankees pitcher knocked home 14 runs in just 71 at bats? Six years earlier he had set a NL record for the most ABs in a season by a pitcher (94) without striking out. Two-run double.

6 Since the end of the Deadball Era in 1919, who had the fewest RBI of any Yankees team ribby leader? Although his total was just 62, he would retire with the most career games played by a Bomber who debuted after the majors expanded—at least he would until Bernie Williams came along. RBI single.

7 When Derek Jeter landed his 627th ribby in 2004, whose record for the most career RBI by a Yankees shortstop did he break? Two-bagger.

8 What Yankees first baseman once hit a dismal .208 but logged a .851 OPS and collected 16 home runs, plus an amazing 45 RBI in just 173 at bats? We'll tack on that he played for every existing AL franchise except Boston during his career and also that he was the first player in ML history to rack up 100 RBI in a season on a sub-.250 batting average. Triple.

9 What Yankees gardener set a post-Deadball Era club record for the most RBI in a season with no home runs when he plated 48 mates while going dingerless? Even with the clue that he did it in the most recent year the Yanks met a team from Illinois in the World Series, this still rates a homer.

10 Which of these ribby makers had the most 100-RBI seasons in a Yankees uniform? Single, plus an extra base if you know which one had the fewest. Mickey Mantle, Thurman Munson, Tommy Henrich, Don Mattingly, Joe Gordon or Paul O'Neill. Single.

> **AB**: 10
> **Hits**: 10
> **Total Bases**: 23
> **RBI**: 7

INNING 3
CY YOUNG SIZZLERS

1 No question that this Gotham hurler deserved the retrospective AL Cy Young for posting a 22-5 record… on the *road*! You read that right. Stop blinking and reason this one out for a single and a RBI for the year.

2 The first Yankee born outside the 50 states to earn a Cy Young vote will net you a single, plus a extra base for his birth place and a RBI for the year.

3 The 1960 Yankees copped 97 wins and the AL pennant but had no Cy Young candidates, chiefly because the team lacked a real staff leader. Who paced the Bombers lackluster mound core that year with 15 wins and was also the club's only hurler to appear in as many as 200 innings? RBI double.

4 Even older Yankees fans nowadays often forget the name of the Yanks first Cy Young Award winner. Beat out this squeeze bunt and bag a single.

5 The first Yankees hurler to collect so much as a single vote for the Cy Young Award got exactly one tally in 1956 but might have won the award if it had existed the previous year when he paced the AL in wins and complete games. Just a single.

6 His .307 BA wouldn't have been in the running for the MVP, but his 21 wins that same year for a certain Yankees World Championship team would have had him in the hunt had there been a Cy Young Award then, especially when the nearest teammate to him had eight fewer wins and eight fewer complete games. For a double, who is he? RBI if you also know his big year.

7 He placed second in the AL with 26 saves and tied for seventh among relievers with 68 strikeouts. However, his 2.17 ERA topped everyone in the league who worked as many as 100 frames and helped earn him a Cy Young in the Bronx Zoo. Another easy bingle.

8 Despite leading the AL with 21 wins for a Yankees world champ, he placed second in that year's Cy Young balloting. Some claimed highway robbery, while others countered that he averaged more than a hit yielded per nine innings, and his 3.87 ERA was just eighth best in the league among qualifiers. This runner-up is worth a single, plus a RBI for the year.

9 Another Yankee who paced the junior circuit in wins but failed to garner the coveted mound trophy went 23-12 and also led the league with nearly 300 innings. It didn't help that they awarded just one Cy Young annually back then and it went to a NLer whose super season prevented our Bombers ace from getting a single vote. RBI single.

10 Which lefty's sparkling 17-4 slate placed him second in that year's AL Cy Young voting behind a man who would be toiling in pinstripes the following season? Take a single for the southpaw, an extra base for the future Bomber and a RBI for the year.

AB: 10
Hits: 10
Total Bases: 14
RBI: 7

INNING 4
ODD COMBINATION
RECORD HOLDERS

1 Among all the ML franchises currently in existence, only one has had a performer who can make the bizarre claim that he owns both its franchise record for the most plate appearances in a season with no home runs and a league record for the most home runs in a season. No trickery on our part here—the statement means exactly what it says. The franchise of course is the Yankees and the sheepish team season record holder with 637 plate appearances and no home runs also proudly possesses the season record for the most home runs in a certain major league. We fancy our chances of slipping this dark one by you well enough to award a two-run homer.

2 The only catcher to log 100 or more assists in a season on four separate occasions as a Yankee also holds the club record for the most assists in a season by a receiver with 180. We'll tell you he was never on a Bombers pennant winner but was the first Yankee to catch 100 games in a season and still holds the club record for the most steals in a season by a backstopper. Two-run homer for his name, plus a third RBI for his big theft season.

3 In 1904, who tied for the New York AL club lead in homers with six and thereupon shared the new team four-bagger record despite setting a negative club mark for the fewest RBI in 400 or more at bats (since broken) when he drove home just 22 runs? A year earlier he had served as a regular outfielder for the Boston Americans in the first 20th century World Series. Homer.

4 When Roger Maris bagged 141 RBI in 1961 on just a .269 BA, whose club record did he break for the most ribbies with a sub-.300 BA? Solo homer.

5 When the decade of the 1920s ended, only 12 men to that point in big league history had hit as many as 20 homers in a season with a sub-.300 BA. Interestingly, three of the 12 achieved this feat (which nowadays is commonplace, of course) with the *same* team in the *same* season. The Yankees are that team. Knowing which Bombers crew it was and the three sluggers involved will net you a double.

6 What hurler holds the Yankees season record for both the most strikeouts (64) and the most innings pitched ($105\frac{1}{3}$) without collecting a win? Obviously a middle reliever, right? Not exactly. This lefty chucker made six starts in his 39 appearances in 1986 and also collected three saves. Surely we've provided enough clues to net you a double.

7 No hitter in major league history has ever collected 100 RBI in a season in which he totaled 20 triples, less than 10 home runs and a sub-.300 BA. The most recent player to come even close to meeting all the criteria fell just one triple shy. He was a Yankee, as you might expect, and his feat came after the end of the Deadball Era, as you might not expect. Though not in the Hall of Fame, his many achievements in pinstripes are well represented in this book. Reason this doozer out and collect a two-run triple, plus an extra ribby for his one-of-a-kind post-Deadball season.

8 This southpaw holds the Yankees season records for both the most wins by a hurler with as many as 20 saves and the most wins by a hurler in less than 120 innings. We'll tell you that at age 34 he led the AL in both saves and appearances—as well as relief wins, natch—the year he set *both* club marks and bestow a RBI double on you for both his name and his magical season. Your shot at a hit winds up in the ditch if you know only his name.

9 He was the most recent Yankees hurler to make more than 10 starts and earn more than 10 saves in the same season. In truth, he's the only Yankee ever to accomplish this feat except for Wilcy Moore. In the process, he set the Bombers all-time season record for the most saves (13) by a hurler who made as many as 15 starts. But we're not finished. The same year our chucker set this odd record, another Yankees staff member nearly matched his one-of-a-kind feat by notching nine saves while making 19 starts! *What* was going on with the Yanks that year? Dunno, but they won a World Championship, and the two flingers finished 1-2 on the club in saves. Name both double-duty moundsmen for a triple, plus a RBI for the year. Sac hit if you know only one of the hurlers.

10 A certain Yankee once held the all-time ML season records for both the most runs and the most walks by a player with a sub-.200 BA. If Tom Tresh's name immediately leapt to your mind, you're on the right track because Tresh later broke our man's record for the most walks. But if you fixed on Tresh because this seems like the sort of thing a swinger with good power having a bad year would do, guess again. The man who still holds the all-time record for the most runs with a sub-.200 BA was none other than the Yanks *leadoff hitter* the year he tallied 84 times and walked 72. Triple, plus two RBI for his weird season.

AB: 10
Hits: 10
Total Bases: 31
RBI: 14

INNING 5
BRAZEN BASE THIEVES

1 Who is the only Yankee to swipe as many as 20 bases in eight consecutive seasons? Born in Los Gatos, California, in 1883, this cat's thievery extended beyond the playing field. See if you can cheat us out of a RBI double.

2 The first Yankees second sacker to snag 40 thefts in consecutive seasons totaled 117 in his three-year Bronx stay and retired with over 400 career steals. Double.

3 Three first sackers have swiped as many as 100 bases while wearing pinstripes. A two-bagger if you nail all three, plus three RBI if you know who stands fourth in thefts among Yankees first baseman with a grand total of 27 and a career high of nine, which came in the same year he rapped a personal best .286 but in just 262 at bats, as he shared duty at the initial sack with Johnny Mize and Johnny Hopp. The clues are there for every expert at least to make an educated guess.

4 Oh, you probably know who stole the most bases of any Yankee in the same season he collected as many as 30 home runs. But a RBI single says you stumble trying to name the Yankee with the most thefts in the same season he hit as many as 40 homers.

5 Here's a true test for hardcore fans and a well-deserved three-bagger. Who is the only man to play as many as 1,000 games with the Yankees prior to expansion and notch fewer than 120 career stolen bases and home runs combined in Bombers garb?

6 Who is the only Yankees infielder to win back-to-back AL theft titles? Double.

7 What Yankee tied a major league record by playing in all 162 games without stealing a base? That season was typical, as he swiped just 14 career sacks across 1,785 games, exclusively in pinstripes. RBI single.

8 Generally, Yankees outfielders have sported more sock than speed. Who was the last Bombers pastureman to steal as many as 30 bases for three straight seasons? This one's no gimme so sprint for two bases.

9 One of these is easy and the other may be tough, but you need both to collect a RBI single. We want to know the only two men that compiled 100 or more career thefts in Yankees garb despite hitting under .250 for all their time in pinstripes.

10 Who is the only Yankees second baseman to swipe as many as 20 bags four straight years? A switch hitter, he spent all but the last 42 of his 1,272 career games with the Bombers but never played on a flag winner. Double.

11 While many stolen-base success rates cannot be verified prior to 1920 due to inconsistent record keeping, whose 43 swipes in 50 tries in the years since 1920 is the highest officially recorded season percentage (.860) by a Bomber in that many attempts? Double and a RBI for the year of his precision thievery.

AB: 11
Hits: 11
Total Bases: 20
RBI: 8

INNING 6
HOME RUN KINGS

1 Who was the first Yankee to win an AL home run crown after VJ Day in 1945? Take a double, plus a RBI for the year.

2 Who was the first player to crank as many as 250 homers in pinstripes without making the Hall of Fame? Adding that he once led the AL in round-trippers reduces this to a RBI single.

3 Who is the only player to slug as many as 25 homers in a season with both the Mets and the Yanks? We can't venture more than a single here.

4 Who posted the highest BA in a season by a Yankees batting title qualifier who hit fewer than 10 homers that year? Regardless of what bat title criteria you apply, he qualifies, belting over .350 on a world champ. Double for him and a RBI for the year.

5 The Yankees began in 1901 as the Baltimore Orioles. The Orioles team home run leader in 1901 repeated as the club leader in 1902 and in 1903 became the only player ever to homer in the uniforms of the original AL Baltimore Orioles and a New York AL entry. Name him for a RBI single.

6 What former Yankee currently holds the big league record for leadoff homers in a season? *Careful*— it's easy to choose the wrong fleet-footed power stick here. Double.

7 Who is the most recent Bomber to lead the club with less than 20 homers in a non-strike season? Although he missed nearly 20 games, his 18 dingers paced the club by one, but his .398 SA was more than 150 points below his career figure. Single for him, plus a ribby for the year.

8 What Yankee is the only player in big league history to crash homers in his first and last career at bats? In 1966, he became the first Bomber to blast a four-bagger in his initial plate appearance. After collecting just one more hit, he exited the Bronx with a mournful .087 BA in 23 at bats. Resurfacing three years later with the Dodgers, he cranked one more seat-reacher before disappearing. Veteran trivia buffs are too familiar with this question to do anything but frown if we awarded more than a double here.

9 In 1990, when the Yanks slipped to last and recorded the worst record (67-95) in the AL, their club leader in homers was an outfielder that had previously topped the junior circuit in dingers. Barring a brain freeze, he's yours for a RBI single.

10 Who became the first slugger to crank 20 homers with two different AL teams in the same season when he poked 20 taters for the Yanks after connecting 21 times with another club earlier that season? RBI single.

> **AB**: 10
> **Hits**: 10
> **Total Bases**: 14
> **RBI**: 6

INNING 7
TEAM TEASERS

1 Here's a routine single for savvy fans that know their history. What Yankees team finished 16 games out of first place despite scoring an AL-leading 1,062 runs and posting a team-record .309 batting average? Garner an extra base if you can name the hurler that led the pitching-thin Yanks that year with a 4.11 ERA.

2 What was the most recent Yankees team to hit fewer than 100 homers in a season? That year they finished fourth in the Eastern Division, 21½ games behind the Orioles. RBI single.

3 The first Yankees club to post a .300 team batting average featured a first baseman that hit just eight home runs and a pitcher that rapped .343 and won 27 games. Use those clues to identify the year for a double, plus an extra base each for the first sacker and the hitting hurler.

4 What was the first Yankees team to win an AL pennant on the last day of the season? The only clue we'll offer up is that Jack Graham led a certain AL club that year in home runs with 24. Double for the year and a RBI for Graham's team.

5 When the Yankees sank to sixth place in 1965, it represented their first sub-.500 finish in 40 years. For a three-run homer, can you pinpoint the last Yankees team prior to the 1925 club to finish below .500?

6 The 1927 Yankees hold the pre-expansion club record for the most wins with 110. Prior to the sensational 1998 crew, what Yanks team came the closest to surpassing the 1927

Murders Row gang? Your clue is that Danny MacFayden went 7-5 for the club but only received a partial World Series share. Triple.

7 What Yankees squad's top winner was a reliever who bagged just 11 victories as they finished last in the AL East while suffering the most losses since their days at Hilltop Park? Just a single for the year, but we'll ante two extra bases for the pen man.

8 What Yankees team featured a record seven pitchers that won in double figures? Which of the seven led the staff in wins and what rookie nearly swelled the total to eight when he went 8-3 with nine complete games and a snazzy 2.41 ERA in 116 innings that probably would have been awarded the AL ERA crown if he had pitched just one more complete game to achieve the unofficial 10 CG minimum then needed to qualify for an ERA title? Single for the team. Take a RBI for the top winner and bag an extra base and two more RBI if you also nab the club's ERA leader.

9 What Bombers club posted the second lowest team batting average in AL history? The 1910 White Sox hit .211, but this Yankees crew smote just .214. Extra base hits were hard to come by too as they slugged a mere .318, which was just a point higher than the previous year. And yet they finished four games above .500! If you're getting a Deadball-Era scent, sniff again. Double.

10 In what year did the Yankees set a record for highest team ERA by a club that won as many as 100 games? They couldn't have done it without a power-loaded lineup that eclipsed the club standard for homers with 242. Single.

AB: 10
Hits: 10
Total Bases: 25
RBI: 9

INNING 8
WHO'D THEY COME UP WITH?

Remember to take two extra RBI for knowing the season each performer here debuted.

1 Johnny Sain. RBI single.

2 Ryne Duren. Two-run homer.

3 Joe Dugan. Two-run homer.

4 Rick Cerone. Triple.

5 Urban Shocker. Two-run homer.

6 Oral Hildebrand. Two-run triple.

7 Fred Stanley. Triple.

8 David Wells. RBI single.

9 Bucky Dent. RBI single.

10 Don Larsen. Triple.

11 Herb Pennock. RBI triple.

12 Lindy McDaniel. Two-run single.

13 Monte Pearson. Solo homer.

> **AB**: 13
> **Hits**: 13
> **Total Bases**: 41
> **RBI**: 35

INNING 9
MASTER MOUNDSMEN

1 In 1975 Catfish Hunter became what is likely to be the last Yankees chucker to hurl as many as 300 innings in a season. What Bombers hurler set the club post-Deadball Era record for innings when he logged 336⅔ frames for a pennant winner and won 27 games despite notching just 70 strikeouts? RBI double.

2 Two Yankees have won 20 games in a season with an ERA of 4.00 or worse. Both were lefties who did it for Bombers flag winners 71 years apart. Double for both, single for one and a RBI for each year.

3 When Terry Mulholland posted a horrendous 6.49 ERA in the 1994 strike season, whose club record did he smash by more than a full run for the highest ERA by a hurler in enough innings to qualify for an ERA crown? Even adding that his given name was Irving still makes this a two-run homer.

4 Who was the first Yankee to be an AL leader or co-leader in wins and play on a World Championship team in the same season? RBI double.

5 Although the Yanks have boasted some fine pitchers, they haven't featured any that came close to fanning as many as 300 batters in a season. What's more, the first Yankee to whiff 200 in consecutive campaigns is still their season K record holder. Cinch single.

6 The only Yankees pitcher to date who bagged a strikeout crown since the majors first expanded in 1961 will net you a single plus a RBI for the year.

7 Who won the fewest games in a season by a Yankee who fanned as many as 200 batters? He whiffed 222 in just 195 innings and posted a 12-6 slate, but would fan 209 the following year while entering the 20-win circle. Single for him and a RBI for the year he struggled for victories.

8 In the 14 seasons prior to expansion (1947–1960), the Yankees won 11 pennants. Just once during that span did they have an outright AL leader in wins. Two-run double for his name.

9 Since the Yankees first flag in 1921, who won the most career games in Yanks garb without ever pitching on a Bombers flag winner? Once a 20-game winner in pinstripes, this lefty was one of the finest control artists in big league history, averaging just 1.73 walks per nine in over 2,000 innings. Two-run single.

10 After Russ Ford led the AL in losses in 1912 with 21, the Yankees would have only one other loop loss leader prior to their shocking cellar finish in 1966. Who was he and what year did he top the AL with 21 defeats? Two-bagger for him and one base for the year.

AB: 10
Hits: 10
Total Bases: 25
RBI: 9

GAME 6

INNING 1
HOME RUN KINGS

1 These days it's common for a player to rap 30 or even 40 homers and hit less than .250, but the Yanks did not have a player who hit even as many as 10 home runs and batted under .250 until 1937—and then they had not one but two such performers! Name both for a two-run triple; sac hit for knowing just one.

2 What slugger led the Yankees in homers the last time Yogi managed them for an entire season? That year our man cracked 27 while playing just five games in the field—which was still the most action he saw with a glove during his three-year Bomber stint. Frozen rope RBI single.

3 The first New York AL club in 1903 had only one former or future big league home run king on its roster. Given the clue that he lost his job that year to Kid Elberfeld, go real, real deep for a three-run dinger.

4 Who blasted 24 homers on just 73 hits for a Bombers World Championship club? Knowing that Torre used him primarily as a DH shaves this to a RBI single.

5 In 1912 the man who led the last place Yanks with six homers tied the then-existing club season dinger record but had an execrable .893 FA to mark him as the last regular outfielder in ML league history to field below .900. Can you name him for a solo homer?

6 In 1963 catcher Elston Howard led the Yanks with 28 homers. It would be a long time until another receiver topped the Yankees in four-baggers. A man who hit 24 while squatting behind the dish 130 times is your ticket to a double, plus a ribby for his year of leadership. The following year he crushed 22 more dingers before his proven futility to reach base and spotty defensive work sent his playing time and stats spiraling downward.

7 When the Mick became the first Yankee other than Ruth to hit 50 homers in a season in 1956, three other Yanks totaled 23 or more taters that year. Name all for a two-run double.

8 What Yankees switch hitter crushed three homers in one game in 2004? Although he connected for 16 round-trippers in only 253 at bats, his .221 average and desolate .297 OBP made him readily expendable. RBI single.

9 Prior to A-Rod, who was the last Yankees third sacker to rap as many as 30 homers in a season? While leading the Bombers in taters that year, he also became the first Pinstriper to crack as many as 30 round-trippers while batting below .250. RBI single, plus an extra base for the year.

10 What aging slugger became the only ML performer prior to Mark McGwire in 2000 to hammer 25 or more homers in less than 300 at bats when he went deep exactly 25 times in just 274 at bats for the 1950 AL flag winners? Double.

> **AB**: 10
> **Hits**: 10
> **Total Bases**: 21
> **RBI**: 11

INNING 2
STELLAR STICKWIELDERS

1 Yankees teammates have finished 1-2 in the AL batting race just once in the club's long history. For a double, name this pair, plus a RBI for the year; no credit for just one player.

2 Several men who played for the Yankees retired with over 3,000 hits. Who was the only one to have already reached that milestone *before* he donned pinstripes? Double.

3 In his initial season with the Yanks he became the first Bomber with as many as 500 at bats to attain a 1.000 OPS since Mickey Mantle in 1964. Rap a single for this slugger whose 41 homers and 112 walks helped put him over the top.

4 It now appears certain that Bernie Williams will not retire with a .300 career BA. Had he done so, he would have become the fifth Yankees centerfielder with as many as 1,000 plate appearances in pinstripes to depart with a .300+ career batting average, counting only games played in center field. Can you name the other four for a two-run homer? We offer such a high prize because, big surprise, one of the four will prove very tough. Sac hit if you know just three.

5 Can you name the lone Yankee to collect as many as 1,000 at bats at two different outfield positions and hit .300+ at each position? Double.

6 This one may cause even experts to take an embarrassing fall. Who holds the Yankees club record for the highest BA with as many as 1,000 plate appearances while playing second base in Yankees garb? Bases-clearing triple.

7 Just a single for knowing the only man to collect as many as 2,000 hits while serving as a catcher wearing pinstripes.

8 The Yankees career record for the highest BA by a catcher who collected as many as 1,000 plate appearances while playing behind the dish belongs to a Hall of Famer and will earn only a single. But it'll net two extra bases if you know what catcher's record he broke.

9 No one knows how many intentional walks Babe Ruth received because major league baseball didn't keep this stat officially until 1955. With that in mind, who holds the Bombers career record for intentional free passes? Double.

10 A two-run homer if you don't wander down the wrong garden path and wind up in the shrubbery when we ask you who the lone hurler is to post a career .300+ BA while collecting as many as 300 plate appearances as a Yankee.

11 Since AL expansion in 1961, who hit the fewest homers in a season by a Yankees batting title qualifier who belted .300? Call us nuts, but we're offering three.

12 The most recent big leaguer to rap 20 or more triples in two consecutive seasons was this Yankee who also became the first player to slap 150 three-baggers in a Bombers uniform. RBI double for this Southern swinger.

AB: 12
Hits: 12
Total Bases: 29
RBI: 9

INNING 3
MEMORABLE MONIKERS

1 Goose. An excuse-me-swing single.

2 The Major. Single.

3 Happy Jack. RBI single.

4 The Tabasco Kid. Triple.

5 What hurler who was nicknamed "Shotgun" killed a man with a pitch in the minors and later pitched on the same Yankees team as Carl Mays? RBI triple.

6 He was christened Alfred and given the middle name of Manuel. What was his nickname?

7 Who was nicknamed "Bobo" on the Yankees first post–World War II pennant winner? RBI double.

8 The nickname of the Yankees hurler that gave up the fewest hits per nine innings pitched in the AL in both 1947 and 1948 will bring a two-run triple.

9 Suitcase. RBI single.

10 The Hit Man. Double.

11 King Kong. Double.

12 A flat-out triple is yours for knowing the only Babe to play for the Yankees whose birth name was Babe. Two ribbies if you also know his nickname.

    AB: 12
    Hits: 12
    Total Bases: 23
    RBI: 9

INNING 4
BULLPEN BLAZERS

1 In 1960, Ernie Broglio of the Cardinals became the last ML pitcher to date both to win 20 games and make as many as 20 relief appearances in the same season. If we tell you that the most recent AL hurler entitled to make the same claim was a Yankee and that he set the ML record for the highest percentage of wins in relief by a 20-game winner when eight of his 20 victories—40%—came as a bullpenner, can you name him for a two-bagger?

2 In 1911 he set a new Yankees record when he appeared 24 times in relief. He later led the NL twice in saves when he was approaching 50. In between he won over 200 games, including eight with the Yanks first flag winner in 1921. Enough there for the shrewd trivia buff to slap a triple off the wall in center.

3 Who came to the Yankees from Washington in 1951 as a starter but left in 1954 as mainly a reliever and a good one? Arriving with Cleveland in 1946 as one of the most heralded young southpaws in the game, he finished with the 1957 Cards and in between cashed three Series checks with the Yanks. Even after learning that he was the first reliever to record the final out in two consecutive Fall Classics, you may find this a tough triple.

4 Although customarily a starter, he came out of the bullpen seven times in the eight occasions he appeared on the mound for the Yankees in fall play and in so doing became the first pitcher to see Series action in each of his first four seasons in the majors. We'll tell you he hurled a shutout in his lone fall start and still cough up a two-run double.

5 What closer did the Yankees let become a free agent after he posted a league-leading 43 saves in 47 chances while averaging more than a strikeout per inning for a Bombers world champ? Single for him, plus a ribby for the year.

6 He came to the Yanks in 1951 with expectations of joining the rotation, but by the time he left for the Bombers Kansas City "farm" team after the 1956 season he was a full-time pen man. Nicknamed "Plowboy," he finished with the 1963 Angels and is today one of the forgotten men from the 1950s, even though he was a part of three World Series teams while with the Bombers. Solo homer.

7 What hurler who once started Game 1 of a World Series against the Yankees later racked up 11 saves and a neat 7-2 record out of the pen on the only Bombers team ever to lose a World Series to a club from Brooklyn? Single for him and a RBI for the year, no credit for just the year.

8 This righty pair set an AL record for combined appearances by a relief duo with 166 but totaled just 7 saves. What's more, they both surpassed the previous *individual* Yankees mark for relief outings in a season as the club bagged 101 victories before faltering notably in the playoffs. Need both workhorses to score a double—zilch for one—plus a RBI for the year.

9 Who appeared in the most games for the Yanks without ever getting a starting assignment? Not once across his 16 big league seasons did he ever toe the rubber at the start of a contest. RBI single.

10 The Yankees record for strikeouts in a season by a bullpenner was set by a man who actually started ten games the year before as a Bomber rookie, one more than he relieved. If we awarded more than a single, you'd laugh us out of the house that Ruth built.

11 Who holds the Yankees record for relief innings in a season? By then, this righty was toiling in his 19th campaign, and went on for two more years elsewhere. Once the co-holder of the Bombers standard for saves in a season, he's good for a single plus a RBI for the year he logged all those relief frames.

AB: 11
Hits: 11
Total Bases: 18
RBI: 8

INNING 5
GOLD GLOVE GOLIATHS

1 One of the finest fielders ever at his position, a certain hot corner man never won a Gold Glove in the AL due to a Hall of Famer's hammerlock on the award during our man's Yankees sojourn. But he did bag one later in the senior circuit, and some argue that he'd be in Cooperstown if he'd been armed with his younger brother's stick. RBI single.

2 What Hall of Famer bagged two straight Gold Gloves in pinstripes but never won the honor in 11 seasons with his previous outfit? The change of scenery and his bat had more to do with his winning than anything else, since many others at his position displayed better range and stronger arms. RBI single.

3 Two Yankees second sackers have amassed over 500 assists in a season. They have much in common in that they both compiled near Hall of Fame credentials with their bats as well as their gloves. We'll toss in that they had their big assist seasons exactly 20 years apart and that both finished their careers wearing the uniforms of other AL teams. Two run triple for both. Just a sac hit for knowing only one.

4 The Yanks career-record-holder for the most assists by an outfielder is in Cooperstown, but you won't make our Hall of Fame if you stumble here and guess the wrong man. Single.

5 Better known for his booming bat, this fly chaser set the Yankees all-time record for the most assists by an outfielder when he threw out 28 runners the year he played in his first of five World Series with the Bombers. His name will add a two-bagger to your column, plus a RBI for his record season.

6 Don Mattingly won nine Gold Gloves while playing for Yankees also-rans. Who was the only first baseman to date to capture the top fielding honor on a Bronx flag winner? It was his lone glove award in nearly 2,000 games at the position. Single, plus a RBI for the year he netted his bullion.

7 He'll always be best known for several unassailable club season pitching marks he set, but we know him too as the Yankees season record holder for the most assists by a moundsman with 166. Single, plus a RBI for the year.

8 After bagging two fielding awards in the NL, this slugging former Big Ten basketball star joined the Bombers and became the first Yankees outfielder to snag five Gold Gloves. Just a single, but grab a RBI for the year he joined the New Yorkers to start his award-winning skein.

9 Post-expansion performers hold all the Yankees third sackers' career fielding marks except one—for the most putouts. What hot corner man who later managed an AL runner-up to a Stengel flag winner owns that mark with 1,220? Double.

10 Which future Bombers team captain bagged two straight Gold Gloves while playing on Yankees world champs in both seasons? Two years before donning pinstripes, he set the season record for assists at his position with another AL club. Double.

AB: 10
Hits: 10
Total Bases: 15
RBI: 8

INNING 6
SHELL-SHOCKED SLINGERS

1 Who posted the following numbers for a Yankees World Champion? A 4-14 record, 6.91 ERA, and over 11 hits and 16 base runners allowed per nine innings. Had he worked just seven more innings he would have qualified for the worst winning percentage in big league history (.222) while toiling for a pennant winner. Stop at first.

2 Billed by the Mets as the next Tom Seaver after making noise at UCLA and in the Texas League, he fell miles short of his early press clippings, going 78-105 with seven teams. From 1990 through 1992, he posted a 13-29 composite in pinstripes, with a 5.12 ERA, including a team record 23 wild pitches in his first season as a Yank. RBI single.

3 What hurler shared the AL lead in wins the season he set the ML record for the most home runs surrendered to one club when the Yankees took him deep 15 times? The lone clue you should need is that both he and his brother won over 200 games, but, unlike his sib, he never pitched for the Yanks. RBI double.

4 Even though he spent most of his years with strong Yankees teams, he holds the AL record for the most career runs surrendered with 2,117. We'll add that his 3.80 career ERA is the highest of any pitcher in the Hall of Fame and grant only a single.

5 The only Yankees hurler prior to AL expansion in 1961 to cough up as many as 25 homers in a season surrendered 25 on the nose in Casey's last season wearing pinstripes. Name him for a two-bagger.

6 Only two Yankees chuckers in the Deadball Era (1901–1919) surrendered more than 10 hits per nine innings while hurling enough frames to qualify for the ERA title. Both did it in the same season and both were known most commonly as Jack. You need both for a triple, and the year they did it will bring two RBI. Sac hit for just one hurler.

7 Who set the Yankees club record for a qualifier when he allowed an incredible 8.22 walks per nine innings in the process of winning 15 games for a World Championship team? Just an infield single since it's clear that he must have had excellent numbers in other areas to survive all those free passes.

8 When Rich Dotson notched 12 wins with a 5.00 ERA in 1988, whose record did he tie for the most victories by a Yankees hurler with an ERA as high as 5.00? Still rates a two-run homer after we announce that he pitched for a Yankees outfit that finished 16 games behind the Mackmen.

9 Hurlers in the Deadball Era who allowed as many as 12.5 baserunners per nine innings usually had very short careers, and this Yankee with his 12.71 baserunners allowed was no exception, exiting the majors after just four seasons (1905–1908), all of them spent in the Gotham. Yet his sudden death in 1909 suggests that there might have been more to his early dismissal than meets the eye, for he holds the all-time ML record by a wide margin for the lowest career ERA (3.06) among all hurlers who were ERA qualifiers at least four times and allowed as many as 12.50 enemy baserunners. It would be piggish of us to keep this gem to ourselves or to award less than a homer.

10 After leading the Bombers with an 18-6 slate, this 6' 7" lefty surrendered 31 homers in just 146 innings for a Piniella crew before getting shipped to the Reds in late August for Bill Gullickson. RBI single, plus an extra base for the year.

11 The first pitcher in AL history to yield four homers in the first inning was a Yankee who fled the premises with two outs after Boston's Rick Burleson, Fred Lynn, Carlton Fisk and George Scott teed off. A single for the man who once held the AL career record for dingers surrendered along with a swarm of positive pitching marks as well.

12 In 2003, while posting an ERA just shy of 6.00, he yielded 11.92 hits per nine frames, the highest season average ever by a Yankees chucker with as many as 150 innings. Commentators noted how unsettled this bony 6' 5" right-hander looked in pinstripes, but you should relax and rap him sharply, like everyone else did, for a clean single.

13 In 1912 the Yanks Ray Caldwell posted the AL's highest ERA by a qualifier at 4.47. Not until the days of Bernie Williams was there a year when another qualifier who pitched an entire season in pinstripes turned that negative trick. After going 16-10 in 1991, this chucker went 12-11 in 1992 with a major-league-worst 4.93 ERA. Like our man in the previous question, he was a 6'5" righty. RBI single.

AB: 13
Hits: 13
Total Bases: 24
RBI: 9

INNING 7
PEERLESS PILOTS

1 What former Yankees player led the club to pennants in each of his first three seasons at their helm but failed to make the Hall of Fame? Single.

2 Who was the lone member of the 1927 Murderers Row team later to serve as a Yankees pilot? Double for him and a RBI for the name of the man who replaced him in the Yankees dugout.

3 What Yankees skipper designated himself as his team's top pinch hitter and proceeded to slap .385 in pinch duty but nevertheless finished in the AL cellar? Even with the clue that he also played a little third base, where he'd previously served as a regular with four different ML teams, experts would howl if we didn't rate this a three-run homer.

4 Who is the only Yankees pilot to fashion 25-win seasons as a hurler in both the NL and the AL? RBI triple.

5 Do you know the three Hall of Famers that can make the claim that they both played for and managed the Yankees in the same season? One base for each.

6 What Yankees coach took over the club's helm when illness forced Miller Huggins to step down near the end of the 1929 season? The clue that he spent most of his career as a shortstop under McGraw should help almost everyone to collect a RBI double.

7 Ever since the Yankees broke through and won their first pennant in 1921, their pilot's seat has been highly coveted and the years spent at their helm have generally helped to inflate the career winning percentage of every man who did so. Do you know the only man to sit in the Yankees dugout for as many as two full seasons since 1921 and yet finish with an overall career winning percentage *below* .500? Solo homer.

8 The only man to grab the Yanks pilot seat immediately after winning a World Championship with another ML team died during the season while at their helm. Double, plus a RBI for the year of his death.

9 Who was the only man to pitch for the Mets and later guide the Yanks? Nine years before he donned pinstripes, this fiery skipper directed a NL world champ. Later, New York called again as he grabbed the Mets helm. Take a single for him and a RBI each for his championship team and the year they won it all.

10 Who was at the controls when the Yanks won their fewest games during a flag-winning season? In the Series, they kicked it into gear and won in five games. Single for the skipper and a RBI for the year.

11 Who is the only man to win a Fall Classic game as a pitcher and later manage a world champ? Although the Yanks were the team he helmed, his mound exploits came exclusively with another club. Double.

12 Besides the Yanks, the nomadic Billy Martin managed four other big league teams. Triple for snagging all of them, a single for three, zip for less.

AB: 12
Hits: 12
Total Bases: 28
RBI: 11

INNING 8
HEROES AND GOATS

1 What Yankees southpaw became a goat in the Bronx but a hero in Flatbush when he was saddled with the loss in the final game of the lone World Series the Dodgers won while the team was based in Brooklyn? He had earlier pitched a complete-game win in the second contest of the 1955 Fall Classic. Triple.

2 Here's a hero turned goat. After going a neat 20-9 with a 2.63 ERA, he dropped 20 decisions the following season as his ERA rose to 3.80 with a Yankees club that posted their worst record in 53 years. Still the most recent Bombers 20-game loser, he's worth a single in your hit column, plus a RBI for his dreadful season.

3 What Yankees performer copped the AL MVP Award in the same season that he hit a meager .095 in a stunning Bombers World Series loss to a team that received a .300 BA from Jimmy Brown, the MVP Yank's counterpart at the same position? Double, plus a RBI for the year.

4 The year the Yankees were swept for the first time in their history in a four-game Fall Classic, they garnered just five walks and scored only four runs. Only one team member hit better than .214 and reached base as many as five times in the four contests as he went 5-for-15 (.333). If we clue you that his last of many Series appearances came four years later with another club when he stroked just .111, can you name the Yanks lone offensive beacon in their first Series whitewash and scamper to a standup double?

5 In his first taste of Series action, this Hall of Fame resident struggled mightily, collecting just one hit in 22 at bats

(.045) as the Yanks lost in six games after capturing the first two. Single for him and a RBI for the year.

6 What rookie led all Yankees hitters in a certain World Series in runs, RBI, home runs, hits, batting average, OBP and slugging average? Knowing that his aggressive baserunning was the catalytic force in the key play in the Series final game should get you in for a double, plus a RBI for the year.

7 What Yankees hurler led the AL in the regular season with a sparkling .768 winning percentage but then was 0-2 in the Yanks first World Series appearance in which they were winless? Double for the hurler, plus a RBI for the year.

8 When Sandy Koufax set a record (since broken) with 15 strikeouts in Game 1 of the 1963 Series, what Yankees part-time infielder fanned ignominiously as a pinch hitter to end the contest? You'll shine here for sure with a two-run double after we tell you he failed again as a pinch hitter later in the Series and was jettisoned by the Bombers after it ended.

9 What Yankee dropped both his World Series starts one year, posting a sky-high 10.00 ERA, with most of the damage coming in his second "effort" where he yielded six runs in two plus innings before Joe Torre mercifully gave him the hook? Single, plus a RBI for the year he blew up.

10 Although Black Sox Lefty Williams lost three games during the 1919 Series, he wasn't trying to win. Hold your nose and name the Yankees reliever who dropped Games 3, 4 and what proved to be the clinching Game 6, helping cement the Bombers collapse against the Dodgers during the 1981 Series. Stinky single.

AB: 10
Hits: 10
Total Bases: 17
RBI: 8

INNING 9
FALL CLASSICS

1 Who was a perfect 6-0 for the Yankees in his six World Series starts in the 1930s? You'll be left at the starting gate if you don't beat out this infield single.

2 Lou Gehrig held down first base in all seven Yankees fall appearances from 1926 through 1938. In the Yankees next seven fall showings, however, from 1939 through 1950, seven different men guarded the initial sack. Three-run homer if you can name all seven in order; solo homer for six; double for five; and a scratch single if you know as many as four of them.

3 A utility infielder and pinch hitter, this journeyman rapped .313 in 163 at bats for the 1981 flag-winning Yanks. Used in place of the injured Bucky Dent, he played in every game of the 1981 postseason but saw action in just 45 games thereafter in pinstripes. RBI double.

4 Snap up a single if you know the only World Series that included both Mickey Mantle and Joe DiMaggio in the Yankees outfield.

5 Numerous Yankees starters won two games in a World Series during the Bombers longest dynasty period, 1947–1964. All but one, however, were veteran hurlers. Can you name the only frosh to cop two wins wearing pinstripes during that 18-year span? Two-run double.

6 Many of the World Series in which the Yankees participated between 1921 and 1960 (the close of the pre-expansion era) were short, often so brief that no Yankees hurler appeared more than once. In 1947 reliever Joe Page became the first Bomber to make as many as four mound appearances in the same Series. Two other Yankees pitchers toed the rubber four times in a Fall Classic later in that span. Both had identical profiles, winning two starts, losing one and collecting a key save in their four appearances. Name both for a solo homer; no credit for just one.

7 Who is the only Yankee to start Game 1 of the World Series after starting *against* the Yanks in the previous year's Fall Classic opener? Rotator cuff woes abruptly ended this lefty's career at age 27 after he'd notched more than twice as many wins as losses in over 150 decisions. RBI single.

8 Which reminds us: Do you know who was the first pitcher to win a game both for and against the Yankees in World Series play? After bagging a victory in three consecutive Fall Classics in pinstripes, he defeated them in relief with a team that lost in seven games. Score a double for him and a RBI for his losing club.

9 The 1960 World Series is famous for the fact that the Pirates won with a staff ERA of 7.11, which was more than double the Yankees staff ERA of 3.54. Within half a run, can you gauge what the Yanks ERA would have been if Whitey Ford's contribution to it were deducted? Double.

10 When the Yanks won four straight World Series between 1936 and 1939, who was the only Bomber to earn victories in each Fall Classic? You might think we're giddy on ballpark brew, but we'll offer three here.

11 What Yankees closer was the first pitcher in Series history to save each of his team's four victories? Knowing that the quartet of winning pitchers was Jimmy Key, Andy Pettitte, David Cone and Graeme Lloyd should easily wet your whistle. Single.

AB: 11
Hits: 11
Total Bases: 23
RBI: 8

GAME 7

INNING 1
RBI RULERS

1 In 1932, Ben Chapman collected 107 RBI while stroking just 10 home runs. In all the years since, who hit the fewest homers by a Yankee (12) in a season when he topped 100 RBI? A .318 average placed him third in the AL that year to offset his lack of pop. Two bases.

2 During the Yanks five-year 1960–1964 flag-winning stretch, Roger Maris led the club in RBI three times and Mickey Mantle once in that span. Who topped the team in the other season? Single.

3 In 1955 what Yankees leadoff hitter rapped 20 homers but managed to log just 53 RBI, the fewest ever by a pre-expansion Bomber with 20 or more dingers? Double.

4 Who collected the most career RBI for the Yankees without ever registering a .300 season BA in his entire career? In 11 years with the Bombers he never batted higher than .276, but he powered his way to 834 RBI and four Yankees pennant winners. Double.

5 The name of the only Yankee to lead the club in RBI during the 1950s whose name was not Berra or Mantle is tough enough to merit a standup triple.

6 Who is the only player to top the Yankees in RBI for seven straight years? He also led or shared the team high in two other seasons. Single.

7 Who was the first Yankee since Joe DiMaggio to drive in 100 runs for five straight seasons? While in pinstripes he reached the century mark on six occasions and twice more elsewhere. Although he never plated more than 118, that figure was good enough to top the NL the year he reached it. Single.

8 The only Yankees club RBI leader to more than double the total of his closest rival was neither Ruth nor Gehrig, but we'll tell you that one of that fabled pair was the club runner-up that year with 68 ribbies and still grant a double if you know who more than doubled the runner-up's total.

9 Which Yankee once led the AL in RBI but later had a season with over 500 plate appearance in which he totaled fewer than 50 ribbies? That proved to be his final campaign as the 49 he plated that year was nearly 100 below his season high. He's a single, plus a RBI for his leadership season.

10 Since AL expansion, who had the most RBI in a season by a Yankee who failed to lead his league? A four-time club leader in ribbies, he placed second behind the Mariners Ken Griffey. Jr., who bested him by six. Single for him and a RBI for the year he fell short.

AB: 10
Hits: 10
Total Bases: 16
RBI: 2

INNING 2
MVP MARVELS

1 The first ALer in the expansion era to hit .300 and total 100 RBI for three straight years was this Yankee who sand-wiched a MVP between his first and third such seasons. Rap a single for him, plus an extra base for correctly nailing the years of his streak.

2 Over the years the Yanks have featured several players who bagged AL MVP awards with other teams. Since the current MVP prize was established in 1931, who is the lone National League MVP winner ever to play for the Bombers? Headfirst triple.

3 Who is the lone Yankees pitcher to capture a MVP Award? RBI double, plus an extra base for the year he won.

4 The closest MVP vote in AL history occurred in 1947. What Yankee won that year by just one vote, 202 to 201? RBI single, plus an extra base if you also know who finished second.

5 Who is the only Yankee to date to be selected MVP in a season when the Bombers failed to qualify for postseason competition? Take a double here, plus a RBI if you know the year he won.

6 Who was the first—and thus far the only—Yankees per-former to capture a MVP Award without having previously received so much as a single MVP vote in his career? Two-run double but only if you also know the year he did it.

7 Elston Howard, the only Yankee to garner a MVP vote in 1967, finished the season with the Red Sox. What was the first year under the current selection system that Yankees players failed to receive a single MVP vote? RBI double.

8 Who is the youngest Yankee to snare a MVP? RBI single, plus an extra base for the year he won.

9 The 1946 season marked the first time since the present award was originated in 1931 that no Yankee finished in the top 10 on the AL MVP ballot. What gardener led all Yankees when he finished 15th with 17 votes? Two-run double.

10 Who were the most recent Yankees teammates to finish 1-2 in the AL MVP voting? The Bombers won it all that season, defeating a club that would not return to the Series until 27 years later. Double for the tandem, an extra base for the year, plus a RBI for the club they beat in the Series.

11 Which Yankee earned MVP votes in four of his first five full seasons but flamed out so quickly that his career ended in the same decade that it began? Near the end of it, all the Bombers could wrangle for him in a straight swap with the Tigers was backup outfielder Ron Woods. Two-bagger.

AB: 11
Hits: 11
Total Bases: 24
RBI: 11

INNING 3
RED-HOT ROOKIES

1 Who set a Yankees yearling record by winning 12 straight games but rode the bench come Series time? His given name was Richard, but this Mississippi chucker went by his unusual middle name. Triple, plus a RBI for the year of his frosh winning streak.

2 Besides Babe Ruth, who was the only regular (minimum 400 at bats) on the 1927 Yankees that did not spend his rookie season in pinstripes? Double.

3 He went nuts out of the gate, becoming the first player (rookie or no) to slug 20 homers in a season while playing in fewer than 80 games. However, he was so disappointing afterward that his .230 career average stands as the sixth lowest among all players with as many as 1,000 at bats in pinstripes. Double, plus a RBI for the year of his rookie outburst.

4 Another frosh who came out swinging was this out-fielder who drilled ten homers in just 67 at bats in his year-ling season and became the first Bomber in history to clout three grand slams in one month. Comparisons to the Mick turned out to be premature, as our man never played more than 94 games in any of his five seasons in pinstripes. Last spied with the Mets, he's a single, plus a RBI for his sensational rookie year.

5 What Yankees Rookie of the Year winner later became the only player since World War II with as many as 500 at bats to hit below .200 in a season? Single for him, plus a RBI for his award-winning season.

6 The first Yankees performer to finish as high as runner-up for Rookie of the Year honors in the AL did not make his hill debut in his freshman season until July 1. Name him for a double.

7 What Yankee would have been the AL's first unanimous selection for the Rookie of the Year Award if a lone contrary vote had not gone to a Red Sox player who had been ruled ineligible for the prize prior to the balloting? RBI single for the Yankee and two more RBI for the controversially ineligible Red Soxer.

8 Who was the most recent Yankees yearling to toss as many as 200 innings in his frosh season? After he'd started one game the previous year, Ralph Houk inserted him into the rotation where he took his medicine for 235 innings while collecting 14 wins and pacing all other big league freshman with a nifty 2.95 ERA. Two bases and a RBI for the year.

9 What Yankees frosh led the AL in winning percentage (.789) and topped all other junior circuit rookies in wins (15) and ERA (2.52)? We'll clue you that he received a no decision in his only start in that year's World Series and add that no freshman trophy existed at the time, but his super season would probably have been eclipsed by Johnny Pesky had there been an official rookie award. Double, plus a RBI for the year.

10 In his frosh season this reliever posted a stunning .875 winning percentage in 16 decisions, plus nine saves. Two years later he tied an AL record by fanning the last eight batters to face him in one game. Bobby Grich, Rod Carew and Fred Lynn were just three of this bespectacled righty's victims as he overpowered the Angels. Take a double for him, plus a RBI for his frosh season.

AB: 10
Hits: 10
Total Bases: 18
RBI: 10

INNING 4
WHO'D THEY COME UP WITH?

Again, our reminder that two extra RBI are earned for each debut year you nail.

1 John Wetteland. RBI single.

2 Hector Lopez. Double.

3 Ralph Terry. RBI triple.

4 Roger Maris. Just a single.

5 Kid Elberfeld. Two-run homer.

6 Mike Kekich. RBI Double.

7 Chris Chambliss. Single.

8 Sad Sam Jones. RBI triple.

9 Luis Arroyo. Solo homer.

10 Goose Gossage. Double.

11 Oscar Gamble. Triple.

12 Jeff Nelson. Single.

    AB: 12
    Hits: 12
    Total Bases: 27
    RBI: 30

INNING 5
STRIKEOUT KINGS

Since the Yankees, rather surprisingly, have a slim history of pitching strikeout kings, we're featuring hitting strikeout kings instead.

1 In his lone season with the Yanks, he sawed the air 137 times, setting a Bombers club record that was later surpassed. A notorious free-swinger, he finished with a then-record 1,757 strikeouts in 1,849 games. RBI single.

2 The first Yankees hitter to lead the AL in whiffs also topped the Bombers that same season in almost every major batting department. In a career that lasted 12 more years, he never again whiffed as many as 70 times in a season and later had a campaign with a Yanks World Championship team in which he bagged 108 RBI while fanning just 28 times. Name the player and the year for an RBI double; sac fly RBI for just the player.

3 At the close of the 2006 season, five men had accumulated as many as 1,000 strikeouts while wearing pinstripes. Two are in the Hall of Fame and none of the five ever played on a team managed by Billy Martin. Can you nail all five for a triple? Single for four; no credit for less.

4 Who is the only Yankees shortstop to lead the AL in whiffs? Learning that he did it two years in a row should help you line a triple here.

5 Which Bomber fanned as many as 100 times in each of his first four full seasons in the majors but nonetheless stroked a nifty .319 over that span while averaging nearly 200 hits per season? Single.

6 What Yankee won a MVP Award the same year he led the AL in both batting strikeouts and errors at his position? Single for him, plus a RBI for the year.

7 Prior to AL expansion in 1961, who were the only two Yankees catchers to fan as many as 50 times in a season? We'll clue you that one of them did it twice, including once just prior to expansion and the other did it while collecting just 290 at bats for the first Yankees team to lose the seventh game of a seven-game World Series. Triple for both men, sac hit if you know only the more recent one.

8 The first Yankee to go down swinging as many as 150 times in a season was this Puerto Rican power hitter who also clubbed 31 homers with 102 RBI that year. Although he debuted as a shortstop with another outfit, he served most of his career in right and as a DH. RBI single.

9 The hitter who holds the present Yankees record for the most whiffs in a season set the mark while rapping .300 with 39 homers and 102 RBI. Take another single for this San Pedro De Macoris product.

10 Who was the first performer to collect as many as 1,000 career Ks while wearing pinstripes exclusively in the post-expansion era? Adding that he whiffed 100 times just once in his career should tell you something about his longevity in Bombers threads. Single.

11 Mickey Mantle led or shared the AL lead in batter strikeouts from 1958 through 1960. However, it would be quite some time until another Yankees hitter topped the junior loop in whiffs. Double for him and a RBI for the year.

AB: 11
Hits: 11
Total Bases: 18
RBI: 4

INNING 6
STELLAR STICKWIELDERS

1 Who was the first Yankees batting title qualifier to slug .600 in a season subsequent to Mickey Mantle in 1962? Double for him plus a RBI for the year.

2 What Yankee holds the AL record for the most total bases in a season by a second baseman? Single and a RBI for the year he set the standard.

3 Fifteen hurlers have collected 100 or more hits while serving as members of the Yankees hill corps. Two-run homer in your column if you know the first Yankees pitcher to crack the 100-hit barrier.

4 Who had the highest career BA (minimum 300 plate appearances) among these pitchers during their service as Yankees hurlers? Don Larsen, Al Orth, Red Ruffing, Eddie Lopat, Carl Mays, Ray Caldwell. Three-bagger.

5 You'll win many a wager betting against any of your cronies being able to name the man who holds the Yankees record for the most singles in a season. We'll add that he hit .315 that year, slapping 205 hits. Neither were his career highs as he previously stroked over .330 elsewhere. Still we remain confident in awarding you a headfirst triple.

6 Only those who really know their Yankees shortstops are likely to pull a RBI triple for the name of the first Bombers shortstop to hit as many as 10 home runs in a season. We'll give a bonus RBI for the year.

7 Catchers don't walk as frequently as other position players. Just one Yankees receiver to date has coaxed as many as

100 free passes in a season, and his name will send you to second.

8 Who holds the Yankees record for doubles in a season by a switch hitter? This one will come as a big surprise to many, so we'll offer a triple.

9 The greatest season for hitters since 1900 is considered to be 1930. That year the Yankees had three stickmen post 1.000+ OPS's with as many as 100 plate appearances. All three are in the Hall of Fame, as perhaps will be you one day if you can name them all for a triple.

10 As the greatest season for hitters since 1900 is considered to be 1930, the 1908 season is judged to be the worst. Tell us the outfielder that led the Yankees in 1908 in both slugging and OPS even though he hit under .300 and failed to rap a single home run, and we'll deposit a grand slam in your account.

11 Who was the last Yankee prior to Don Mattingly to stroke 200 hits in a season? That year he also set a team season record for at bats that lasted for four decades. Take a double for him and an extra base for the player who topped his at bat mark.

AB: 11
Hits: 11
Total Bases: 26
RBI: 6

INNING 7
HOME RUN KINGS

1 Who was the first man to hit a home run wearing a New York AL uniform? Every self-respecting Yankees fan will net an easy double here.

2 Who was the first man to club as many as 20 career home runs in a New York AL uniform? Surprise yourself and nail a RBI triple.

3 Name the four parks that swat king Babe Ruth called home during his ML career and bag a stand-up double. Earn an extra two bases by naming them in the *order* in which Ruth called them home.

4 While both leagues boasted scads of big boppers with 30+ homers between 1998 and 2000, the Yanks won three straight championships despite featuring a 30-tater man just once. Who was he for a single?

5 Whose record of 53 for the most career home runs as a Yankee did Babe Ruth smash in his very first season with the Bombers? RBI single.

6 Who holds the Yankees record for the most homers in his final big league season? He pounded as many as 20 seat-reachers six times in pinstripes, but blackjack must have been his game as he poked exactly 21 three times. Last seen in Series play, he's a single, plus a RBI for the year he departed after his third and last 21-dinger season in Bombers livery.

7 If the DH rule remains on the books in the AL, who stands to be the last Yankees pitcher ever to hit as many as four home runs in a season? We'll add that he was no slouch with a bat and collected both his first and his last career hit with an AL franchise that got its start in Milwaukee in 1901. Triple.

8 Who is the only player since expansion to powder as many as 20 homers in seven straight seasons while sporting pinstripes? Not once did this lefty swinger ever hit 40 during his lengthy career, but he did top 30 twice in the Bronx. RBI single.

9 Derek Jeter leads all Yankees shortstops in career homers by a wide margin. For a pinch double, whose old record of 94 did he break?

10 Who hit the fewest homers among players with at least 5,000 at bats in pinstripes? He debuted with the Bombers as a teenager and never played elsewhere. In parts of 12 seasons up top, he connected for just 34 seat-reachers in 5,386 at bats but twice stroked .300 as a regular. Double.

> **AB**: 10
> **Hits**: 10
> **Total Bases**: 23
> **RBI**: 4

INNING 8
MASTER MOUNDSMEN

1 In 1945 several pitchers—Paul Derringer for one—hurled 154 or more innings in what was to be their final ML seasons, as the many hurlers who had been called to military duty during World War II returned to the game the following year. Between 1946 and the first expansion year in 1961 only four hurlers logged 154 innings (or what in 1951 became officially the minimum number of innings needed to qualify for an ERA title) in their final ML seasons. One was Jim Wilson with the 1958 White Sox. The other three, amazingly at one time during the 1946–1960 span, were all teammates on a World Championship Yankees club. Name all three, plus the year they were teammates, and bag a home run. Double if you know only two, and no credit for less.

2 We'll turn our backs and allow you to beat out a bunt single by naming the only chucker to win 20 games in a season for both the Mets and the Yanks.

3 What hurler shattered both the Yankees season club record and the post-Deadball ERA ML season record for the fewest hits per nine innings (5.74) in the first season he logged enough innings to qualify for an ERA crown? Prior to 1968, his .183 opponents' batting average the year in question also ranked as the AL's lowest since the end of the Deadball Era. Double.

4 Incredibly only one pitcher who began his ML career prior to 1939 ranks among the top 100 all-time in career home runs surrendered. Perhaps even more incredibly, he spent most of his career in Yankees garb. Why do we make 1939 our parameter year? Because that season marked the debut of the *second* pitcher in ML history to cough up as many as 300 career home runs. Interestingly, he wore a Yankees uniform at one point in his career, as did Robin Roberts, the first ML slinger to be tagged for 300 gopher balls. But unlike Roberts, whose Bombers stay in 1962 was so brief that he didn't even get into a game, the second man saw World Series action with the Yanks, in 1958 after participating in his only other Fall Classic a dozen years earlier. Homer if you can identify both the Yankees hurlers under discussion here in addition to Roberts. Single if you know just one.

5 In his second tour of duty with the Yanks, this veteran lefty experienced the finest season of his career by going 15-5 with a league-leading 2.46 ERA. That year he also showed his versatility, making 24 relief appearances along with his 17 starts. Those 24 relief appearances are the most by an AL ERA leader since Diego Segui logged 28 in 1970. RBI single.

6 Three pitchers who won as many as 300 games wore pinstripes at one point in their careers. Take a double for all three, a single for two, but zip for less.

7 Who was the only Yankees hurler to win 20 games more than twice during the team's unparalleled 1946–1964 dynasty? Not the easiest single in the book.

8 Among pitchers who debuted since expansion, who is the only hurler to log as many as 1,000 innings with the Yankees and post a career ERA below 3.00? Two-run single.

9 In 1942, Tiny Bonham became the first Pinstriper to average less than a walk per nine innings while working as many as 200 frames. However, a certain rotund southpaw who issued just 20 free passes in 213 innings for a stingy 0.85 ratio later topped Bonham's mark of 0.96. His name's worth a single.

10 Ron Guidry posted an ERA below 3.00 on three occasions during the 1970s. Only one other Yankees ERA qualifier did it more than once during that decade. Unfortunately an arm injury helped finish his career before he turned 30. Adding that he shares the same first and last name with a later-day NL reliever who became the first modern hurler to appear in over half his team's games for three years straight still makes this a double.

11 What Yankees mound master became the first big league hurler to win as many as 20 games in a season without logging a single complete game? In five seasons with the Yanks, he rarely finished what he began, going the distance just three times in 157 starting assignments. Single for him, plus a RBI for the record year.

AB: 11
Hits: 11
Total Bases: 18
RBI: 5

INNING 9
FALL CLASSICS

1 Two men in addition to the Babe played on all five Yankees World Series entries in the 1920s. Name the two and bag a double; a swinging strikeout for anything less than both.

2 What Yankees batter was given a last-ditch life when Brooklyn catcher Mickey Owen missed his swinging third strike with two outs in the ninth inning of Game 4 of the 1941 World Series, allowing him to reach base where he later scored the tying run? Just a single.

3 Forgotten in the hoopla of Reggie's Series three-homer game is the fact that this starter bagged the victory that night after defeating Lasorda's gang in Game 3, going the distance in both contests with a 2.50 composite Series ERA. RBI single.

4 Between 1921 and 1939, the Yankees appeared in 10 World Series but used only four men as their leadoff hitters in those 10 Series. Three of the four played the same position. What was it? Single for the position and a RBI for each of the three Series leadoff hitters that played it, plus an extra base for the lone member of the quartet of Series leadoff hitters that played a different position.

5 Knowing the losing pitcher that Don Larsen faced in his perfect game in the 1956 World Series will bring you only a single. But two RBI come your way if you also know the most prominent thing Larsen's and our man's career paths had in common.

6 What Yankee was the first player to score ten runs in a Series that lasted six games? Named the Fall Classic MVP, he'd already copped that honor with another world champ. Gift-wrapped single.

7 Here's a performer who truly rejuvenated his career upon joining the Bombers. After batting .203 with another AL outfit, he excelled in his first season with the Yanks, striking an even .300 with 19 homers and 98 RBI. Far from finished, he topped off his reclamation campaign in the Fall Classic with a team-leading .471 BA, two homers and six RBI, plus Series MVP honors. RBI single.

8 In parts of nine seasons a certain light-hitting middle infielder hit just 12 homers in 1,584 at bats, including a mere one in 217 at bats in 1976. Nevertheless, this Alabama native was the only Yankee to go deep in the 1976 Series. Double.

9 Alfonso Soriano played every game at second base for the Yanks during both the 2001 and 2003 Series with one exception. Do you remember the Dominican switch hitter Torre employed in 2003 at the keystone sack in the starting lineup for Game 5 against the Marlins? RBI double.

10 A two-run homer is yours for the name of the only man to play in a World Series game under both Bucky Harris and the lone pilot to manage two AL teams *other than* the Yankees in World Series play between 1947 and 1964. We'll add that he hit a towering .750 for Bucky and played every inning of every game for the other skip. Two bases for him and an extra base for the skipper, but down to a sac hit for knowing only one of the pair.

AB: 10
Hits: 10
Total Bases: 15
RBI: 8

ANSWER SECTION

GAME 1

Inning 1: RED-HOT ROOKIES

1. Dave Righetti, 1981.
2. Gil McDougald and Minnie Minoso.
3. Thurman Munson, 1970.
4. Rollie Sheldon.
5. Bob Grim, 1954.
6. Russ Ford, 26 in 1910.
7. Stan Bahnsen, 1968.
8. Wilcy Moore, 1927.
9. Brian Fisher, 1985.
10. Earle Combs, .342 in 1925.

Inning 2: WHAT WAS THEIR REAL HANDLE?

1. George Herman Ruth.
2. George, the same as his son.
3. Edward.
4. Richard.
5. Robert.
6. Charles.
7. Edward.
8. William.
9. William.
10. Wilson.
11. Michael.
12. Horace.

Inning 3: MASTER MOUNDSMEN

1. Jack Chesbro, 41 wins in 1904.
2. Tommy John, 1979–1980.
3. Bob Turley, 210 in 1955.
4. Red Ruffing who tossed over 200 frames from 1931 through 1940, and logged as many as 20 complete games from 1936 through 1940.

5. Catfish Hunter, 1975.
6. Ray Caldwell.
7. Jimmy Key.
8. Sal Maglie.
9. Lefty Gomez.
10. Ed Figueroa, 1978.

Inning 4: GOLD GLOVE GOLIATHS

1. Bobby Shantz.
2. Norm Siebern, 1958.
3. Roy White, 1971.
4. Lou Gehrig, 1937–1938.
5. Bobby Murcer, 1972.
6. Hal Chase.
7. Frank "Home Run" Baker, who saw Series action with the A's in 1911 and 1912 against the Giants in the Polo Grounds.
8. Bobby Richardson at second base.
9. Everett Scott.
10. Phil Rizzuto and Jerry Coleman, 1950.

Inning 5: RBI RULERS

1. Not Bernie, it was Jorge Posada with 101.
2. Reggie Jackson from 1977 through 1980.
3. Paul O'Neill.
4. Babe Ruth, with 137 in 1920.
5. Graig Nettles 1977.
6. Jimmy Williams.
7. Hal Chase, with 76 in 1906.
8. Lyn Lary, 1931.
9. Wally Pipp.
10. Derek Jeter in 1999 and Danny Tartabull in 1993.

Inning 6: TEAM TEASERS

1. 1978, Ron Guidry and Ed Figueroa.
2. 1969, after Mickey Mantle's retirement.
3. 1908, Kid Elberfeld.
4. 1914, Roger Peckinpaugh.
5. 1906, Chicago White Sox, as Cleveland won the team Triple Crown.
6. 1947, Bill Bevens.
7. 1954, but there was no postseason for the Yanks—despite winning 103 games they finished second to Cleveland!

8. 1959, Mickey Mantle.

9. Mickey Rivers had 43, Willie Randolph 37, and Roy White 31 in 1976.

10. 1941, Joe DiMaggio 30, Tommy Henrich 31, Charlie Keller 33.

Inning 7: HOME RUN KINGS

1. Wally Pipp, with 12 in 1916.
2. Herm McFarland.
3. Frank "Home Run" Baker.
4. Graig Nettles, who belted 32 in 1976 and 37 in 1977.
5. Tommy Henrich.
6. Bill Skowron, Dodgers, 1963.
7. Tommy Byrne.
8. Kevin Maas, 406 games.
9. Roy Smalley, 1982, Twins.
10. Lou Gehrig, 1936, the Indians.

Inning 8: ALL IN THE FAMILY

1. Jason and Jeremy Giambi, who teamed with Oakland 2000–2001.
2. Bobby and Billy Shantz, 1960.
3. Bob and Irish Meusel, 1921.
4. Angel Aragon and son Jack.
5. Brothers Felipe and Matty teamed on the 1973 Yanks, their other sib was Jesus, and Moises (Felipe's son) hit .355 for the 2000 Astros.
6. John and Charlie Ganzel, Detroit Wolverines.
7. Charlie and Hal Keller.
8. George and Ed Pipgras.
9. Wally and Bobby Schang.
10. Faye and "Marvelous Marv" Throneberry.
11. Jesse Tannehill and brother Lee.

Inning 9: FALL CLASSICS

1. Derek Jeter and Bernie Williams.
2. Carl Mays.
3. Elmer Miller.
4. Mike Stanton.
5. Leo Durocher, in 1928 as a player and in both 1941 and 1951 as a manager.
6. Lonnie Frey, 1939 Reds.

7. Ron Guidry.

8. Aaron Ward.

9. Chad Curtis.

10. Brian Doyle and Bucky Dent.

11. Benny Bengough, Wally Schang, Johnny Grabowski, Fred Hofmann and Pat Collins.

GAME 2

Inning 1: STELLAR STICKWIELDERS

1. Babe Ruth, 1924.

2. Snuffy Stirnweiss, 1944–1945.

3. Bernie Williams, 1999.

4. Joe DiMaggio, 1939.

5. Willie Randolph, led the AL in 1980.

6. John Knight, .312 in 1910.

7. Jerry Mumphrey.

8. Not Lou Gehrig whose best was 99—it was Don Mattingly who totaled 101 in 1985–1986.

9. Tony Lazzeri, .354 in 1929.

10. Tom Sturdivant, 1956.

11. Joe Sewell, three Ks in 1932.

Inning 2: HEROES AND GOATS

1. Babe Ruth, with Bob Meusel batting.

2. Thurman Munson in 1976.

3. Billy Martin.

4. Jay Witasick.

5. Jack Chesbro.

6. Mariano Duncan, 1996 against the Braves.

7. Bob Turley, 1958.

8. Tony Kubek, 1958 and 1963.

9. Bobby Richardson, 1964, 13 hits.

10. Art Ditmar.

Inning 3: CY YOUNG SIZZLERS

1. Whitey Ford.

2. Allie Reynolds.

3. Ron Guidry in 1978.

4. Roger Clemens was 39 when he won in 2001.

5. Spud Chandler, 1943.

6. Lefty Gomez, 1937.
7. Ernie Bonham, 1942.
8. Mel Stottlemyre, 164 wins.
9. Al Orth, 1906.
10. Sparky Lyle, 1972 when he received three votes.

Inning 4: BRAZEN BASE THIEVES

1. Bobby Bonds, 1975.
2. Ben Chapman 1931–1933.
3. Jeff Sweeney.
4. Phil Rizzuto with 18 in 1949, two behind Bob Dillinger.
5. Snuffy Stirnweiss, 1944–1945; in 1944 he tied teammate Johnny Lindell for the lead in triples.
6. Fritz Maisel, 1914.
7. Babe Ruth.
8. Ben Chapman, 1931.
9. Rickey Henderson stole 93 bases in 106 attempts in 1988.
10. Dave Fultz.
11. Mickey Mantle, who stole at least one bag in each of his 18 seasons in pinstripes.

Inning 5: WHO'D THEY COME UP WITH?

1. Cleveland in 1961.
2. Pittsburgh in 1899.
3. Baltimore in 1964.
4. Boston Red Sox in 1924.
5. Minnesota in 1967.
6. Boston Red Sox in 1915.
7. St. Louis Cardinals in 1936.
8. California Angels in 1974.
9. Cincinnati in 1936.
10. Chicago White Sox in 1944.
11. Pittsburgh in 1975.
12. Cleveland in 1963.

Inning 6: FAMOUS FEATS

1. Tony Lazzeri.
2. Ray Caldwell.
3. Johnny Lindell.
4. Myril Hoag.
5. Vic Raschi.

6. Spud Chandler on July 26, 1940.

7. Marcus Thames.

8. David Wells, 1998.

9. Elston Howard.

10. Rick Rhoden.

11. Tony Lazzeri, won the PCL home run crown in 1925 with a then Organized Baseball record 60 home runs.

Inning 7: MEMORABLE MONIKERS

1. Phil Rizzuto.

2. Tony Lazzeri.

3. Hensley Meulens.

4. Bob Roth.

5. Mickey—he was named after Mickey Cochrane.

6. Fred Stanley.

7. Spurgeon Chander.

8. Dick Tidrow.

9. Gene Michael.

10. George Selkirk.

11. Ron Guidry, who was also dubbed "Gator."

12. Clarence Marshall.

Inning 8: FORGOTTEN UNFORGETTABLES

1. Roy Sherid, 1929–1931.

2. Hope you didn't slip and say Ron Blomberg because it's Jim Ray Hart.

3. Duke Carmel.

4. Hersh Martin, nine in 1944.

5. Ben Paschal.

6. Tex Neuer.

7. Chet Trail.

8. Wade Taylor.

9. Tommy Byrne.

10. Jack Reed.

11. Bob Cerv.

Inning 9: RBI RULERS

1. Despite his carousing and atrocious dietary habits, Babe Ruth remains the oldest Yankee to do so, with 103 in 1933 at age 38.

2. Alvaro Espinoza, 1990.

3. John Anderson, 82 in 1904.

4. Bob Meusel, 1925.

5. His own, 175 in 1927.

6. Babe Ruth, Lou Gehrig and Joe DiMaggio.

7. Yogi Berra, 1949.

8. George Selkirk.

9. Ray Caldwell.

10. Joe Gordon did it three times.

GAME 3

Inning 1: BULLPEN BLAZERS

1. Carl Mays.

2. Wilcy Moore.

3. Johnny Murphy.

4. Mike Stanton.

5. Jay Howell, fanned 106 as a reliever, plus three in his one start in 1984.

6. Joe Page.

7. Ron Davis in 1980.

8. Jim Turner, later the Yankees pitching coach.

9. Steve Farr in 1992.

10. Walter Clarkson, bother of John.

11. Goose Gossage, 1978.

Inning 2: HOME RUN KINGS

1. Joe DiMaggio, 1937 hit 46 homers at age 22.

2. Charlie Keller, 1939.

3. Not the Scooter; it's Willie Randolph.

4. Joe Gordon and Tommy Henrich.

5. Graig Nettles, who cracked his dingers in 1974–1975 during Yankee Stadium's renovation.

6. Kid Elberfeld.

7. Frank "Home Run" Baker.

8. Glenallen Hill, 2000.

9. Nick Etten, with 22 in 1944.

10. John McGraw's resignation as the New York Giants manager due to ill health.

Inning 3: MASTER MOUNDSMEN

1. Red Ruffing, 190 in 1932.

2. 45 years, Bob Turley in 1955.

3. Ray Caldwell.

4. T'was Babe Ruth.

5. Carl Mays, who won 26 in 1920 and 27 in 1921.

6. Herb Pennock, 17 in 1925 with a 2.96 ERA and just 16 wins.

7. George Uhle.

8. 1908, Joe Lake 22 and Jack Chesbro 20.

9. Tommy John, 1979.

10. Jack Powell.

Inning 4: NO-HIT NUGGETS

1. Tom Hughes.

2. Sad Sam Jones.

3. Allie Reynolds, 1951.

4. Dwight Gooden, 1996.

5. Cookie Lavagetto.

6. Bob Feller, on May 30, 1946.

7. Dave Righetti, age 24, 1983.

8. How many took the bait and guessed Ruth? The correct answer is none of them.

9. Ray Caldwell.

10. George Mogridge.

11. Jim Abbott in 1993.

Inning 5: WHAT WAS THEIR REAL HANDLE?

1. Carroll.

2. James.

3. John.

4. Harold.

5. Frank.

6. Up to tricks again—Reynolds's real first name was Allie.

7. Bernabe.

8. Walter.

9. Herold, but full credit for Harold.

10. Vernon.

11. Constantino.

12. Russell.

Inning 6: CIRCLING THE GLOBE

1. George Selkirk.

2. Chili Davis, Jamaica.

3. Pedro Gonzalez.

4. Rugger Ardizoia.

5. Art Jorgens.

6. Irish McIveen.

7. Henry Kingman.

8. Jimmy Austin.

9. Graeme Lloyd.

10. Hideki Irabu with 13 in 1998.

11. Willie Miranda.

12. Hensley Meulens.

Inning 7: STELLAR STICKWIELDERS

1. Babe Ruth, hit .393 in 1923; lost to Harry Heilmann.

2. Mickey Mantle hit a career high .365 in 1957 and lost the bat title to none other than Ted Williams.

3. Did you fan by guessing Mantle or Maris? Don Mattingly posted a league-topping 388 total bases in 1985.

4. Jerry Coleman, 1952.

5. Rickey Henderson, 146 in 1985 and 130 in 1986.

6. Roger Maris, .620 in 1961, the year he hit 61.

7. Lou Gehrig, 18 triples and 47 homers in 1927.

8. Birdie Cree, 1911.

9. Chris Chambliss in 1976 and 1977.

10. Bob Meusel, 338 in 1925 when he hit .290.

11. Mark Koenig.

Inning 8: RBI RULERS

1. Carl Mays, 1921.

2. Billy Johnson, 95 in 1947.

3. You said Mickey? It was Bernie Williams who's done it five times, one more than Mantle.

4. Thurman Munson, 1975 and Don Mattingly, 1986.

5. Alfonso Soriano, 2002.

6. Hideki Matsui.

7. Nick Etten.

8. Wally Pipp.

9. Willie Keeler.

10. Bill Dickey, 1936.

11. Tony Lazzeri, 9 homers in 1930.

Inning 9: RED-HOT ROOKIES

1. Left field; he didn't move to center field until his second year.

2. Vic Raschi.

3. Charlie Keller had a .447 OBP in 1939 when he walked 81 times in just 398 at bats.

4. Bob Grim, 1954.

5. Billy Johnson.

6. Orlando Hernandez in 1998.

7. Fritz Peterson, 1966.

8. Derek Jeter in 1996.

9. Lou Gehrig, 20 in 1925.

10. Jim Beattie.

GAME 4

Inning 1: JACK OF ALL TRADES

1. Joe Pepitone and Mickey Mantle.

2. Aaron Ward.

3. Gil McDougald.

4. Chuck Knoblauch.

5. Roy Hartzell, pronounced the same as Topsy Hartsel.

6. Yogi Berra.

7. Elston Howard, 1956.

8. Jack Saltzgaver.

9. Wid Conroy, Bid McPhee.

10. Ken Griffey, Sr., 1983.

11. Babe Ruth and Johnny Lindell.

12. Tom Tresh, shortstop; his outfield Gold Glove came in 1965.

Inning 2: HOME RUN KINGS

1. Enos Slaughter, slugged two Series homers with the Cards, one of them against the Yanks in 1942, and one for the Bombers in 1956.

2. Joe Pepitone, 1966.

3. Tom Tresh, who led in 1966.

4. None other than Hal Chase, the same Hal Chase that holds the club season record for the most at bats without a home run.

5. Jim Lemon of Washington.

6. Jim Spencer, 1979.

7. Yogi Berra.

8. Charlie Keller.

9. Johnny Blanchard.

10. Mickey Mantle in 1958 and 1960.

Inning 3: TUMULTUOUS TRADES

1. Kid Elberfeld.
2. The Yanks received Sparky Lyle for Danny Cater.
3. Willie McGee.
4. Graig Nettles.
5. Herb Pennock.
6. Lou Piniella.
7. Allie Reynolds
8. Jay Buhner.
9. Bob Turley and Don Larsen.
10. Ralph Terry.
11. Monte Pearson.
12. Fred "Crime Dog" McGriff.

Inning 4: WHAT WAS THEIR REAL HANDLE?

1. Richard.
2. George.
3. Arthur.
4. William.
5. Lawrence.
6. George.
7. Edward.
8. James.
9. Ladislaw.
10. Ellsworth.
11. Albert.
12. Leavitt.

Inning 5: MVP MARVELS

1. Birdie Cree.
2. No, not Babe Ruth—it was Joe Bush.
3. Lou Gehrig not only received the most votes of any Yankee but won the award.
4. Elston Howard collected 140 hits in 1963 and defeated the Tigers Al Kaline.
5. Lou Gehrig, 1936.
6. Alex Rodriguez won the AL MVP with the Yankees in 2005 and with the Rangers in 2003.
7. Johnny Allen, 1932.
8. Elliott Maddox.
9. Eddie Mayo of the pennant-winning Tigers.

10. Third base and left field.

11. Mariano Duncan, garnered 26 votes in 1996.

Inning 6: MOMENTS TO REMEMBER

1. Casey Stengel.

2. Mike McNally.

3. Paul O'Neill, the Reds Tom Browning in 1988.

4. Sorry if you guessed Herb Pennock—it was Bob Shawkey.

5. Jack Chesbro; the other Hall of Fame hurler was manager Clark Griffith.

6. Mickey Mantle on April 17, 1951.

7. Mike Stanley on August 10, 1995.

8. Mel Stottlemyre.

9. Spec Shea.

10. Ron Guidry.

11. Chuck Knoblauch.

Inning 7: PEERLESS PILOTS

1. Dick Howser, 1980.

2. Yogi Berra, in 1964 and 1984.

3. Bucky Harris, 1948.

4. Clyde King.

5. Clark Griffith, 1903.

6. George Stallings.

7. Frank Chance.

8. Joe McCarthy, 1932.

9. Roger Peckinpaugh finished the 1914 season as the youngest manager in AL history and topped the club in homers with three.

10. Joe Torre, 2002–2004.

11. Stump Merrill and Buck Showalter.

12. Bill Virdon, who guided the Yanks at Shea Stadium in 1974–1975 while their home park was being renovated.

Inning 8: RED-HOT ROOKIES

1. The lofty reward should have steered you off Harry Simpson who was not a rookie when he joined the Yanks in 1957; the second rook was catcher Jesse Gonder but not until 1960.

2. Jerry Priddy.

3. Hideki Matsui, 2003.

4. Bill Burbach.

5. Al Downing in 1963.

6. Leo Durocher, member of the 1928 Yankees and manager of the 1951 New York Giants.

7. Alfonso Soriano, 2001.

8. Andy Pettitte in 1995.

9. Bill Skowron.

10. Joe Lake, with 22 in 1908.

Inning 9: FALL CLASSICS

1. Waite Hoyt.

2. Lou Piniella.

3. George Pipgras.

4. Cedric Durst.

5. Cecil Fielder, who hit .391.

6. Pete Alexander, Tony Lazzeri, Jesse Haines (the win) and Waite Hoyt (the loss).

7. Yogi Berra.

8. Johnny Allen.

9. Ralph Terry in 1962.

10. Jake Powell.

11. Bob Turley in 1956 and 1958. Orlando Hernandez in 1999 and 2000.

GAME 5

Inning 1: ALL IN THE FAMILY

1. Ray Boone, grandfather of Aaron.

2. Bill and George Dickey, catcher.

3. Braggo and Frank Roth, who debuted with the 1903 Phillies; the other four Yanks home run kings were Wally Pipp, Babe Ruth, Bob Meusel and Frank Baker.

4. Tom and Mike Tresh.

5. Charlie Hemphill, brother Frank.

6. Phil and Joe Niekro in 1985.

7. Graig and Jim Nettles.

8. Jose and Ozzie Canseco.

9. Jose Cruz (Sr. and Jr.) and his brothers Tommy and Hector.

10. Pascual, Melido and Carlos Perez.

11. Roy Smalley, Jr., and Roy Smalley III.

Inning 2: RBI RULERS

1. Johnny Mize, 1950.

2. Bobby Murcer.

3. Tony Lazzeri.
4. Roger Peckinpaugh, 1914.
5. Johnny Sain.
6. Roy White in 1968.
7. You said Rizzuto? It was a different *paisano*—Frankie Crosetti.
8. Eddie Robinson in 1955.
9. Myril Hoag in 1938.
10. Don Mattingly with five, Tommy Henrich with just one.

Inning 3: CY YOUNG SIZZLERS

1. Jack Chesbro, 1904 when he bagged 41 wins.
2. Ed Figueroa, Puerto Rico, 1976.
3. Art Ditmar.
4. Bob Turley, who in 1958 became the first AL honoree
5. Whitey Ford.
6. Red Ruffing, 1939.
7. Sparky Lyle.
8. Andy Pettitte, 1996.
9. Ralph Terry in 1962.
10. Jimmy Key and David Cone, 1994.

Inning 4: ODD COMBO ACHIEVEMENTS

1. Hal Chase led the Federal League in 1915 with a loop-record 17 home runs.
2. Jeff Sweeney, 1914.
3. Patsy Dougherty.
4. Bob Meusel, 1925.
5. 1925 Yankees, done by Babe Ruth, Bob Meusel and Lou Gehrig.
6. Bob Shirley.
7. Wally Pipp, 1924.
8. Luis Arroyo, 1961 when he won 15 and saved 27.
9. Allie Reynolds and Johnny Sain in 1952.
10. Frankie Crosetti, 1940.

Inning 5: BRAZEN BASE THIEVES

1. Hal Chase.
2. Steve Sax in 1989 and 1990.
3. Hal Chase, Wally Pipp and Lou Gehrig all had over 100 steals; fourth on the club with a huge drop-off is Joe Collins.
4. Oops, did you say Mickey Mantle? It's A-Rod with 21 thefts to go with his league-leading 48 homers in 2005.

5. Third sacker Red Rolfe.
6. Snuffy Stirnweiss, 1944–1945.
7. Don Mattingly in 1986.
8. Roberto Kelly, 1989–1991.
9. Fritz Maisel and Frankie Crosetti.
10. Horace Clarke.
11. Mickey Rivers, 1976.

Inning 6: HOME RUN KINGS
1. Mickey Mantle, in 1955 with 37.
2. Graig Nettles.
3. Robin Ventura, 32 for the 1999 Mets, and 27 for the 2002 Yankees.
4. Earle Combs, 1927 hit .356, with just six homers.
5. Jimmy Williams.
6. Alfonso Soriano.
7. Mickey Mantle, 1968.
8. John Miller.
9. Jesse Barfield.
10. David Justice played for the Tribe earlier in 2000.

Inning 7: TEAM TEASERS
1. 1930, George Pipgras.
2. 1971, they hit 97.
3. 1921, Wally Pipp and Carl Mays.
4. 1949, St. Louis Browns.
5. 1918 Yankees.
6. 1932 with 107 wins.
7. 1990, Lee Guetterman.
8. 1939, Red Ruffing, wins, and Marius Russo, ERA.
9. 1968.
10. 2004, with a 4.69 ERA.

Inning 8: WHO'D THEY COME UP WITH?
1. Boston Braves, 1942.
2. Baltimore Orioles, 1954.
3. Philadelphia A's, 1917.
4. Indians, 1975.
5. Experts should have immediately become suspicious that we're awarding the ultimate prize here, because Shocker is most often associated with the St. Louis Browns. Actually he debuted with the 1916 Yankees!

6. Indians, 1931.
7. Seattle Pilots, 1969.
8. Blue Jays, 1987.
9. White Sox, 1973.
10. Browns, 1953.
11. Philadelphia A's, 1912.
12. Cardinals, 1955.
13. Indians, 1932.

Inning 9: MASTER MOUNDSMEN

1. Carl Mays 1921.
2. Lefty Gomez in 1932 and Andy Pettitte in 2003.
3. Bump Hadley, 5.31 in 1937.
4. Waite Hoyt with 22 wins in 1927 tied Ted Lyons for the AL lead.
5. Ron Guidry, who fanned 248 and 201 in 1978 and 1979 respectively.
6. Al Downing, 1964.
7. David Cone, 1997.
8. Bob Turley in 1958 with 22.
9. Fritz Peterson, 109
10. Sam Jones, 1925.

GAME 6

Inning 1: HOME RUN KINGS

1. Tony Lazzeri with 14 and Frankie Crosetti with 11.
2. Don Baylor, 1984.
3. Herman Long.
4. Darryl Strawberry in 1998.
5. Guy Zinn.
6. Matt Nokes, 1991.
7. Yogi Berra hit 30, Hank Bauer poled 26, and Bill Skowron added 23.
8. Tony Clark.
9. Mike Pagliarulo, who hit 32 homers and batted .234 in 1987.
10. Johnny Mize.

Inning 2: STELLAR STICKWIELDERS

1. Don Mattingly edged out Dave Winfield .343 to .340 in 1985.

2. Paul Waner, who played briefly with the Yanks in 1944 and 1945.

3. Jason Giambi posted a 1.034 OPS in 2002.

4. Joe DiMaggio, Earle Combs, Mickey Mantle with .310 counting only his games as a centerfielder, and our special kudos if you got Whitey Witt.

5. Babe Ruth, left field and right field.

6. Del Pratt, .295.

7. Yogi Berra.

8. Bill Dickey with .313 broke Wally Schang's mark of .297.

9. Don Mattingly, with 136, 10 more than the Mick.

10. Ruffing you say? Wrong we say. It's Joe Bush.

11. Wade Boggs, with two in 1993 when he hit .302 and again in 1996 when he stroked .311.

12. Earle Combs in 1927–1928.

Inning 3: MEMORABLE MONIKERS

1. Rich Gossage.

2. Ralph Houk.

3. Jack Chesbro.

4. Norman "Kid" Elberfeld.

5. Tom "Shotgun" Rodgers.

6. Billy Martin.

7. Bobo Newsom.

8. Frank "Spec" Shea.

9. Harry Simpson.

10. Mike Easler.

11. Dave Kingman was "Kong," but only Charlie Keller sported the full moniker.

12. Third sacker Loren Babe (1952–1953) known as "Bee Bee."

Inning 4: BULLPEN BLAZERS

1. Bob Grim, 1954.

2. Jack Quinn.

3. Bob Kuzava.

4. Johnny Kucks

5. John Wetteland, 1996.

6. Tom Morgan.

7. Jim Konstanty, 1955.

8. Paul Quantrill (86) and Tom Gordon (80), 2004.

9. Sparky Lyle, who relieved 420 times for the Yanks.

10. Mariano Rivera fanned 130 exclusively in relief in 1996.

11. Lindy McDaniel in 1973 logged 138⅓ of his 160 total innings in relief.

Inning 5: GOLD GLOVE GOLIATHS

1. Clete Boyer, Ken's brother.
2. Wade Boggs, at third base in 1994 and 1995.
3. Del Pratt, 1920 and Joe Gordon, 1940.
4. It's Babe Ruth with 181 as an outfielder in pinstripes.
5. Bob Meusel, 1921.
6. Chris Chambliss, 1978.
7. Jack Chesbro, 1904.
8. Dave Winfield, 1982.
9. Red Rolfe, piloted Detroit in 1950.
10. Graig Nettles, set the assists mark with Cleveland.

Inning 6: SHELL-SHOCKED SLINGERS

1. David Cone, 2000.
2. Tim Leary.
3. Jim Perry, 1960.
4. Red Ruffing.
5. Art Ditmar.
6. Jack Quinn and Jack Warhop, 1911.
7. Tommy Byrne, 1949, the year he also logged a Yankees club-record low 5.74 hits per nine innings.
8. Roy Sherid, 5.18 in 1930.
9. Bill Hogg.
10. Dennis Rasmussen, 1987
11. Catfish Hunter on June 17, 1977.
12. Jeff Weaver.
13. Scott Sanderson.

Inning 7: PEERLESS PILOTS

1. Ralph Houk, 1961–1963.
2. Bob Shawkey, Joe McCarthy.
3. Harry Wolverton in 1912.
4. Caught you again if you guessed Clark Griffith—it was Bill Donovan.
5. Clark Griffith, Frank Chance and Bill Dickey—Chance of course is the toughie.
6. Art Fletcher.
7. Bucky Harris, who nevertheless made the Hall of Fame.
8. Johnny Keane in 1966.
9. Dallas Green, Phillies 1980.

10. Joe Torre in 2000, when they won just 87.

11. Bob Lemon with Cleveland.

12. Twins, Tigers, Rangers, and A's.

Inning 8: HEROES AND GOATS

1. You got burned, literally, if you guessed Whitey Ford; it was Tommy Byrne.

2. Mel Stottlemyre, 1966.

3. Joe Gordon, 1942.

4. Elston Howard in 1963, played in the 1967 Series with the Red Sox.

5. Dave Winfield, 1981.

6. Charlie Keller crashed into Cincinnati catcher Ernie Lombardi in the 10th inning of Game 4 of the 1939 Series.

7. Joe Bush, 1922 when they averted a four-game sweep by tying one contest.

8. Harry Bright.

9. Andy Pettitte, 2001.

10. George Frazier.

Inning 9: FALL CLASSICS

1. Lefty Gomez.

2. Babe Dahlgren 1939, Johnny Sturm 1941, Buddy Hassett 1942, Nick Etten 1943, George McQuinn 1947, Tommy Henrich 1949, and Johnny Mize 1950.

3. Larry Milbourne.

4. 1951, DiMag's last season.

5. Did you guess Mel Stottlemyre? Sorry—it was Frank Shea.

6. Allie Reynolds, 1952; Bob Turley, 1958.

7. Don Gullet.

8. Don Larsen, San Francisco Giants in 1962.

9. 5.02.

10. We don't ante three-baggers that easily. It's Monte Pearson.

11. John Wetteland in 1996.

GAME 7

Inning 1: RBI RULERS

1. Thurman Munson, 1975.

2. Joe Pepitone, with 89 in 1963.

3. Hank Bauer.

4. Graig Nettles.

5. Hector Lopez topped the team with 93 in 1959.

6. Lou Gehrig, 1930–1936.

7. Dave Winfield.

8. Wally Pipp, who drove in 138 runs in 1925 to outpace Gehrig.

9. Don Mattingly, 1985.

10. Tino Martinez, in 1997 drove in 141.

Inning 2: MVP MARVELS

1. Thurman Munson, 1975–1977.

2. Jim Konstanty of the 1950 Phillies also played for the Yanks in 1954–1956.

3. Spud Chandler, 1943.

4. Joe DiMaggio, Ted Williams.

5. Yogi Berra, 1954.

6. Roger Maris, 1960.

7. 1990, when they placed last in the AL East at 67-95.

8. Don Mattingly, 24 years, 5 months and 16 days by season's end in 1985.

9. Charlie Keller.

10. Mickey Mantle and Bobby Richardson in 1962, the Giants.

11. Tom Tresh.

Inning 3: RED-HOT ROOKIES

1. Atley Donald, 1938.

2. Joe Dugan.

3. Kevin Maas, 1991.

4. Shane Spencer, 1998.

5. Tom Tresh, 1962; he batted .195 in 1968.

6. Whitey Ford.

7. Tony Kubek and Frank Malzone in 1957.

8. Doc Medich, 1973.

9. Hank Borowy, 1942.

10. Ron Davis, 1979.

Inning 4: WHO'D THEY COME UP WITH?

1. Dodgers, 1989.

2. Kansas City A's, 1955.

3. We're up to one of our tricks—Terry returned to the Yanks in 1959 after debuting with them in 1956 and then being traded to the Kansas City A's the following year to complete his major league apprenticeship.

4. Indians, 1957.

5. Phillies, 1898.

6. Dodgers, 1965.

7. Indians, 1971.

8. Indians, 1914.

9. Cardinals, 1955.

10. White Sox 1972.

11. Cubs, 1969.

12. Mariners, 1992.

Inning 5: STRIKEOUT KINGS

1. Bobby Bonds in 1975.

2. Wally Pipp, 1916.

3. Babe Ruth, Mickey Mantle, Bernie Williams, Derek Jeter and Jorge Posada.

4. Frankie Crosetti, 1937–1938.

5. Derek Jeter, from 1996–1999.

6. Joe Gordon, 1942.

7. Elston Howard and Pat Collins.

8. Danny Tartabull fanned 156 times in 1993.

9. Alfonso Soriano, 157 Ks in 2002.

10. Bernie Williams.

11. Jason Giambi fanned 140 times in 2003.

Inning 6: STELLAR STICKWIELDERS

1. Alex Rodriguez, .610, 2005.

2. Alfonso Soriano, in 2002 totaled 381.

3. Al Orth.

4. How many steered clear of Ruffing but bit on Lopat? The answer is Carl Mays who hit .279.

5. Steve Sax hit 171 singles in 1989.

6. Lyn Lary, 1931.

7. Jorge Posada drew 107 walks in 2000.

8. Jorge Posada strikes again with 40 in 2002.

9. Babe Ruth, Lou Gehrig, and the 100 plate appearances should have warned you we were up to something—the third man is pitcher Red Ruffing.

10. Charlie Hemphill.

11. Bobby Richardson who stroked 209 hits in 692 at bats in 1962, and Alfonso Soriano who totaled 696 at bats in 2002.

Inning 7: HOME RUN KINGS

1. John Ganzel.

2. Hal Chase.

3. Did that offer of an extra two bases give you pause? It should have. The correct order is Fenway Park, Braves Field, Polo Grounds, Yankee Stadium—the Red Sox used Braves Field for the 1915 World Series, and the Babe, of course, later finished his career there.

4. Bernie Williams, 30 in 2000.

5. Wally Pipp.

6. Paul O'Neill, 2001.

7. Don Larsen, Browns and Orioles.

8. Graig Nettles.

9. Frankie Crosetti.

10. Bobby Richardson.

Inning 8: MASTER MOUNDSMEN

1. Allie Reynolds, Bill Bevens and Johnny Lindell, 1947.

2. David Cone.

3. Tommy Byrne, 1949.

4. Red Ruffing and Murry Dickson.

5. Rudy May in 1980.

6. Roger Clemens, 1999–2003, Phil Niekro, 1984–1985 and Gaylord Perry, 1980.

7. Vic Raschi, won 21 each year from 1949–1951.

8. Mel Stottlemyre, 2.97.

9. David Wells, 2003.

10. Steve Kline, who posted a 2.96 ERA in 1971 and 2.40 in 1972.

11. Roger Clemens, 2001.

Inning 9: FALL CLASSICS

1. Bob Meusel and Waite Hoyt.

2. Tommy Henrich.

3. Mike Torrez.

4. Center field with Elmer Miller, Whitey Witt and Earle Combs; shortstop Frankie Crosetti.

5. Sal Maglie. He and Larsen were the only two men ever to be teammates of Mickey Mantle, Duke Snider and Willie Mays during their ML careers.

6. Reggie Jackson in 1977.

7. Scott Brosius in 1998.

8. Jim Mason.

9. Enrique Wilson.

10. Sherm Lollar, 1947 Yankees under Harris and 1959 White Sox under Al Lopez.

YOUR SCORE

Okay, now add up all your scores and find out where you stand.

AB:
H:
Total Bases:
RBI:

BA:
SA:

ABOUT THE AUTHORS

David Nemec is one of the best-selling baseball writers in the United States. His *Great Baseball Feats, Facts and Firsts* has sold over 700,000 copies in various editions, the most recent of which was coauthored with **Scott Flatow**. Between them, Nemec and Flatow have won ten National Trivia Contests sponsored by the Society for American Baseball Research.